ENOUGH is ENOUGH

A Call to Christian Involvement

D1113671

ENOUGH is ENOUGH

A Call to Christian Involvement

Rick Scarborough

P.O. Box 1000
Pearland, TX 77588
281-485-6633
www.visionamerica.org

ENOUGH is ENOUGH
A Call to Christian Involvement

Cover and book design: Lee Fredrickson
Printed in the United States of America

For additional copies or a list of other resources from Vision America call 281-485-6633 or write to P.O. Box 1000, Pearland, Texas, 77588-1000. Discounts for quantities are available.Unless otherwise noted, all Scripture is from the NIV.

Dedication

This book is dedicated to three men of God, whom I greatly esteem...

Dr. Freddie Gage, who has the gift of encouragement. His life and his work both challenge me to excellence.

Dr. J. Harold Smith, who came to our church to preach a revival and invested himself in my life. I count it my privilege to call him, friend.

Dr. Jerry Falwell, an example to the world of what God can do with a yielded life.

All three men have the common threads of courage, conviction and consistency running through their lives.

Acknowledgment

This book is the product of many people who have played significant roles in my personal development and the completion of this work.

Above all others, I thank my wife of 25 years, Tommye Glyn. Since December 27, 1970, she has stood at my side, holding my hand and my heart. She is my closest friend. She has helped me forge this book into reality.

I thank my children for their sacrificial love, overlooking my flaws and giving me the exalted status of "Dad." Misty, Richard and Kathryn are my joy.

I thank my mom, dad and sister for their unwavering confidence all these years.

Apart from my immediate family, no one played a bigger role in getting this manuscript to press than Danette and Randy Hufstetler. Danette is the most capable and professional assistant I have ever known. She patiently typed and prayed over every word of *Enough is Enough*. Randy is a Spirit-led attorney, loyal friend and faithful deacon in our church. They make a great team together.

I owe a debt of gratitude to my church family, deacons, and staff for enabling me to take the time to write *Enough is Enough*. The member of First Baptist Church, Pearland are special people, whom I love with all my heart. Two members of my staff, Rod Compton and Scott Tollett, deserve special recognition for covering my bases while I was away on a 30-day leave of absence to write the book. They are champions.

One deacon stands out above the list...Jerry Richardson. He is a Spirit-filled computer genius who contributed hours of research to this project. He is also a cherished friend.

In God's Sovereignty, He directed me to Liberty House Publishers for my first venture into this arena. Lee Fredrickson and Jim Combs have been gifts of God in the process. They are consummate professionals with a spirit of servanthood. Thank you.

Finally, I thank my God for pushing me from my comfort zone to do something I've known for some time He wanted me to do. I acknowledge that He and He alone is ultimately due all praise to any good that has been accomplished.

Rick Scarborough
Author

Table of contents

Preface

I live in Pearland, Texas, where I have the privilege of pastoring First Baptist Church. Pearland is an all-American city. Nestled on the southeast edge of the greater Houston Metroplex, Pearland offers all the advantages that a major metropolitan city affords while still maintaining a small town feel. We have our own police force, school system and city government. Visitors driving through Pearland are amazed to see beautiful new homes and commercial development in one direction, and livestock grazing in the opposite direction.

I love living in Pearland. You can travel twenty minutes north and be in downtown Houston. You can travel forty minutes south and be on the coast. In fifteen minutes you can be at Hobby Airport, one of Houston's two airport facilities, and fly anywhere in the world. It is a great place to live.

In July of 1993, one of the families in our church was contacted by the editors of *Life* Magazine. They soon discovered that the editors of *Life* were running a special feature on "Material World." After an exhaustive computer analysis, they developed a profile of an average American family. Their data included such pertinent information as number of children, ages of children, years of marriage, household income, etc. They were looking for the epitome of an all-American family. Their search brought them to this family who belonged to First Baptist Church, Pearland.

In July of 1994, this family was featured in an article in *Life* magazine. When asked to reveal the most cherished item they possessed, they chose their family Bible. I have never been prouder of a deacon or his family. Pearland is an average American community filled with average American people.

In the spring of 1992, I visited our local high school to attend a high school assembly that was promoted as an AIDS Awareness Assembly. Throughout the presentation, I became increasingly angered over what I was hearing. Finally, after about thirty minutes, I decided, "That is it! I have had it...Enough is enough!"

A week later, I shared with our whole congregation what I had heard. Corporately, they rose up and said... "Enough is Enough." We proceeded to mobilize the Christian community in Pearland, and do something about a school assembly that we believed was wrong. In the months that followed, Christians made an impact in Pearland for the glory of God.

Dear Reader, how bad will it have to get in this country before you finally decide; "Enough is Enough?" Look around. America is disintegrating right before our eyes. Christians can no longer afford the luxury of assuming that someone else will do something. Not until we rise up as a unified body of believers and say "Enough is Enough" will there be a real revival.

This book is a "Call To Christian Involvement." There are three main sections that address America: past, present, and future. My prayer for this book is that it will motivate tens of thousands of believers, nationwide, to stand up and say "Enough is Enough."

—Rick Scarborough

Dr. Paige Patterson says...

While many books have appeared evaluating the present moral and religious scene in America, very few have been published which exhibit succinctness, carefully measured objectivity, and advice that grows out of experience rather than theory. In my estimation, not only the Christian public, but also the general public that desires a safe and moral society in which to live will find Rick Scarborough's *Enough is Enough: A Call To Christian Involvement* to be a most succinct and measured activist response.

Pastor Rick Scarborough's own experience in Pearland, Texas, of facing an initially hostile environment exhibits something I have believed to be true for a long time. His experience, plus the book that grows out of it, is Exhibit A that the general public has simply acceded to the shrill and illogical perspectives presented by a radical few, who, by the noise they make, sometimes appear to be the majority. When someone raises a different standard, such as Rick Scarborough and the members of his church, then thoughtful people (even unbelievers) find themselves convinced by the logic of the position and tend to hasten to surround the standard and support an appropriate view.

Enough is Enough is an invaluable resource, if for no other reason than due to Section Three - "The Hedge Is Restored As The American Dream Is Reborn." Not only has Rick Scarborough succeeded in bringing together, in one readable volume, a mass of information relating to an analysis of our society today, but he has also succeeded in demonstrating exactly how it is that a gracious, thoughtful, Christlike believing protest can be launched in such a way as to effectively change the face of a community. My prayer to God is that every pastor and every layperson who cares about the future of his children and grandchildren will read this book, be blessed by it, and be activated by it. God bless Rick Scarborough for sharing his heart and mind in this wonderfully perceptive monograph.

Dr. Paige Patterson,
President
Southeastern Baptist Theological Seminary
Wake Forest, North Carolina

Dr. James T. Draper says...

Out of the chaos of public policy and procedures has emerged a fresh new wind of sanity that can herald a new day for the communities of America. Rick Scarborough has penned a remarkable volume in *Enough is Enough: A Call To Christian Involvement.* In this thoroughly biblical and sensible approach to appropriate Christian activism in the life of our society, Rick has pointed the way to a healthy balance in the moral and ethical dilemmas of our day.

Having grown up in the Houston area, I know Pearland, Texas, very well. I have preached in that city from time to time over more than 40 years. I went to high school just a few miles from that community. I know the obstacles that were facing the Christians in that city as they sought to bring appropriate change in their public policies educationally and governmentally. This book chronicles the challenge and strategy engaged and carefully reveals the remarkable results of Christian involvement in that Houston suburb.

This is a message that needs to be trumpeted across this land. God has clearly given us the mandate to be light in a darkened world, to be salt in an insipid and corrupt society. *Enough is Enough* raises God's standard and gives simple insights into how this can be done. This is not a book about theory, but has been proven in the arena of combat and conflict. The results are victorious and God-honoring. Every Christian who cares about the future of our society and our nation, should read this significant book.

Dr. James T. Draper, Jr.
President
Southern Baptist Sunday School Board
Former president of the Southern Baptist Convention
Nashville, Tennessee

SECTION ONE

The Hedge Is Raised As The American Dream Is Born

Introduction

Nehemiah is one of the most gripping and encouraging books in all the Bible. I would encourage every pastor in America to spend time with Nehemiah. In 1993, while entrenched in a battle to reestablish a moral foundation in the city where I am pastoring, God led me to preach a series of messages from the book of Nehemiah. There is no contemporary book on the market today that presents a more compelling tale of leadership and its role in society, than this thirteen chapter book.

The book opens with Nehemiah fasting and praying with a broken heart, (three indispensable ingredients in restoring a nation) before the Lord of heaven. Early in the book of Nehemiah, we discover him to be a devout man of prayer. We soon discover he is equally a man of action. Woven throughout the book, God graphically illustrates the principle that He will act if we will act.

Influence And Power Are Gifts To Be Used

Nehemiah, who has a position of rank and importance in the palace of the King, realizes something many Christians in post-Christian America have forgotten; position and influence are power. They are never granted to Christians for ego inflation, personal gratification, or self-exaltation among other Christians. Neither are they granted so that a believer can validate the depth of his humility by never wielding them. Position and influence achieve their highest purpose when a godly man, through honest means, achieves them, while recognizing God's sovereignty in his success. The obscure, bold prayer of Jabez recorded in I Chronicles 4: 9 has long impressed me:

> Jabez was more honorable than his brothers...And Jabez called on the God of Israel saying, "Oh, that you would bless me indeed, and enlarge my territory, that your hand would be with me and that you would keep me from evil that I may not grieve me! (KJV)

Jabez boldly prayed for money, power, and influence, which is what "enlarged territory" meant in his culture. Jabez had it right, for he essentially prayed:

> Lord, don't remove your hand from me in the process. Let me

understand in my spirit who it is that is responsible for any success I enjoy so that I might not grieve you by succumbing to pride.

Jabez understood that success often gives birth to self-sufficiency in those who achieve it, so he prayed for understanding.

I have heard some condemn this type of praying. There are those that have fallen victim of extreme pietism, who hold suspect any believer who achieves career success and the resulting material blessings that may accompany that success. I am much more interested with how God views this bold prayer than I am with what the critics have to say. Look at God's response, "So God granted Him what he requested."

What a powerful affirmation! There is no doubt in my mind that many, perhaps thousands of people, benefited from the boldness of Jabez' prayer, for he was "more honorable than his brethren."

Nehemiah was a man of great position and influence in King Artaxerxes' palace. He had a comfortable life and secure employment as the "cupbearer" of the king (at least, as long as no one sought to poison the king). Yet he chose to risk falling into disfavor with the king and lose it all in order to save his beloved Jerusalem, the City of God. When the king, noticing his sad countenance, (a recipe for imprisonment or execution for a servant) inquired why he was so sorrowful, Nehemiah did two things. He breathed a silent prayer to the King of Kings, and he answered aloud to the King of Persia (Nehemiah. 2: 4).

"Why should my face not look sad when the city where my fathers are buried lies in ruins and its gates have been destroyed by fire" (Nehemiah. 2:3). He then proceeded to request permission to go to Jerusalem and rebuild the walls.

I am certain everyone who heard this request stood aghast. Why would a pagan king grant such a request? Who does Nehemiah think he is to even make such a request? Look at Jerusalem. Its days of glory were all gone. The walls had been torn down and its people conquered and demoralized. All but a remnant had been carried away into captivity. Besides, others had tried and failed. Jerusalem was finished, Judah had fallen.

God Was Listening

The Scripture states: "The king's heart is in the hand of the Lord; He directs it like a watercourse wherever He pleases" (Proverbs 21:1). When Nehemiah recognized that King Artaxerxes was open to him, he made a series of bold requests:

1. Let me return to the city and rebuild the walls;

2. Grant me letters with your signature that will assure me safe passage through hostile territory;

3. And grant me letters that will instruct the keeper of your personal, forests to give me adequate supplies of timber for the construction.

To an onlooker it would appear that Nehemiah had incredible courage. (We call that "guts" where I come from.) In fact, what Nehemiah had was an incredible God. Read carefully how Nehemiah recorded what transpired:

> "And because the gracious hand of my God was upon me, the king granted my requests. So I went to the governors of Trans-Euphrates and gave them the king's letters. The king had also sent army officers and cavalry with me" (Nehemiah. 2:8-9).

There can be no doubt that Nehemiah knew who was in charge. This was not the testimony of a man about to film a documentary detailing how he charmed a king and saved a nation. His humility and dependence on God freed God to be Himself. Not only did God grant Nehemiah's request, He granted far more than he requested. God led the king to provide an army to accompany and assist his servant. Hundreds of years later, the Apostle Paul testified to the Ephesian church that his God was a God of abundant provision:

> "Now to him who is able to do immeasurably more than all we ask or imagine, according to his power that is at work in us, to him be all glory in the church and in Christ Jesus throughout all generations, forever and ever! Amen" (Ephesians 3: 20-21).

Despite continuous opposition both from within his own ranks and from the enemies of God, Nehemiah, with single-hearted devotion, pursued his calling to rebuild the walls of Jerusalem and to restore the nation of Judah. He endured personal attacks ranging from slander and false accusations, to plots on his own life. The book of Nehemiah is a classic study of what the man of God can expect when he enters the public arena where Satan's dominion is strong. It is not an arena for sissies, but we must never forget that our God is an awesome God who responds to those who seek to honor Him. Nehemiah was a man who stood up to be counted because he decided "Enough is Enough."

Joshua And Caleb Were Students Of History

Standing at the threshold of the promised land, Moses sent twelve brave men into the land to explore it and bring back a report. All twelve men saw the obstacles that stood between the people of God and their ultimate goal of occupying the land and receiving His promised blessings. Ten of the men saw only the high walls around heavily fortified cities, and the fierce, warrior giants that occupied those cities. They reported to Moses:

> "We can't attack those people; they are stronger than we are." Of themselves they said, "We seemed like grasshoppers in our own eyes, and we looked the same to them" (Numbers 13:31-33).

Joshua and Caleb brought back a very different report. Caleb silenced the people and said, "We should go up and take possession of the land for we can certainly do it" (Numbers 13:30).

How do you explain the difference between the two reports? Joshua and Caleb were students of history. They lived their lives in context. As they explored Canaan, they not only saw the obstacles, they also saw the potential for great good. They remembered their past. They remembered how God listened to the cries of His children and miraculously delivered over 2,000,000 impoverished and powerless slaves from the hands of the wicked Pharaoh and his colossal war machine. They remembered the plagues. They remembered the night of the Passover. They remembered the crossing of the Red Sea. These memories put it all in perspective. For them, the issue was not the size and strength of the enemy, but rather the size and strength of their God.

Many Have Avoided The Conflict

Today, the challenge Christians face in America is the same. There are legions of Christians in America who, for a multitude of reasons have withdrawn from the conflict that rages in our nation. Two opposing worldviews are vying for control of our culture. On the one hand are those who believe there is no God. They deny the veracity of the Bible and reject any concept of life after death. They believe that man is inherently good and that he is the captain of his own fate.

Opposing this view are those who believe in the God of Scripture and accept the Bible as His revelation for living. They believe that man is inherently sinful and dependent on God both in the here and now, and the hereafter. The two views are in direct conflict with each other as they compete in the arenas of public policy. Many Christians dislike conflict and therefore avoid the confrontation.

We have that option, but we must consider the cost. The ten spies who brought back their "majority" report concluded that living in Kadesh was better than dying in Canaan. They never even considered the option of living in Canaan with its vast resources. The selfishness of their decision was staggering. In opting for immediate personal comfort, they were forfeiting future wealth and blessings. Surely they were not considering the future of their children in their decision,

The most compelling reason I hear for avoiding the potential conflict we face in America, is a view that tugs at my own belief system. There are many sincere and faithful Christians who believe that we are in the last days, and that the events that have unfolded during the last thirty years are simply a part of God's plan. They believe America and, for that matter, the world, are irreversibly marching toward Armageddon. The Church, so the theory goes, should concentrate on saving souls and should withdraw from an increasingly corrupt world.

That mind-set has already resulted in one period of profound darkness. Not until Martin Luther left the safe haven of the monastery and got involved in the politics of a decadent church did the darkness end. I confess my struggle with this issue. I confess my fear that I may be "kicking against the goads" of God's sovereign will when I advocate Christian activism. Whether it entails marching in front of an abortion clinic, which I occasionally do, or breaking a law which I believe is in violation of the commandments of God, I do not want to waste my energies on lesser things than the best. During the Republican National Convention in Houston, Texas, in 1992, an unelected Judge, Ms. Eileen O'Neil, appointed by Governor Ann Richards, issued an illicit court order, which in effect, made a public sidewalk in Houston, Texas to be a "Gospel-Free Zone," by declaring that no protesters could march within 100 feet of a planned parenthood clinic. When I heard that a state court order had been issued restricting my constitutional rights to assemble and to preach the Gospel, I determined to obey God rather than man. I will never forget the fear that gripped my heart as a group of preachers stood on that sidewalk in Houston, Texas, and preached the

Gospel of the Lord Jesus, while an angry mob of pro-abortionists shouted threats at us. As I preached, a Federal Marshall read the court order forbidding me to do so. When I finished, I fully expected to be arrested, however, I was allowed to walk back to a crowd of supporters without incident. Later that day, a number of other pro-lifers were arrested.

The Barbarians Are Ransacking The Cities

I have finally concluded that God has chosen to conceal certain details of "last days" events. No man can fully understand and know all of God's plans for the future, but we can distinguish, with the aid of his Holy Spirit, right from wrong. We do know that it's never right to do wrong, and it's never wrong to do right. Christians, in large measure, have been far too silent for far too long on far too many issues. Our silence on these issues and withdrawal from the conflict has enabled Satan and his forces to steal our country. The walls of morality and decency have been destroyed and the Barbarians are now ransacking the cities. We can no longer afford to hide in the safety of our Christian schools, our Christian television networks, our Christian church buildings and our Christian resorts. We have a responsibility to be salt and light in the world.

Can we succeed in turning America back to Christ? We can if God wills it. We must follow the pattern of Nehemiah who both prayed and acted. Like they often say in East Texas, we must "pray and grab a hoe," and head for the garden. When the first Christians came to America they faced hostile natives and hostile climates. They were underfunded, outmanned, and in uncharted territory. They were farmers by trade, not warriors, but they prevailed because they depended on God and God came to their aid.

David Knew His History

Like Joshua and Caleb, we need to review our history. We need to be reminded to cease looking at the obstacles, and instead, see the greatness of our God. When young David visited the battlefield where Goliath was humiliating God's army, he demanded an explanation. While a whole army decided Goliath was too big to hit, David decided he was too big to miss. As David stood before King Saul about to face Goliath, he rehearsed his history for all to hear:

"...When a lion or a bear came and carried off a sheep from the flock, I went after it, struck it and rescued the sheep from its mouth. When it turned on me, I seized it by its hair, struck it and killed it. Your servant has killed both the lion and the bear; this uncircumcised Philistine will be like one of them because he has defied the armies of the living God. The Lord who delivered me from the paw of the lion and the paw of the bear will deliver me from the hand of the Philistine" (I. Samuel 16: 34-37).

It's time for a David to stand up to the Goliath of secular humanism in America and cut off the head of the wicked giant. When David saw Goliath taunting the armies of Israel, he said, "Enough is Enough." When will you decide, "Enough is Enough?"

"Men are qualified for civil liberty in exact proportion to their disposition to put moral chains upon their own appetites."

-Edmund Burke

Chapter One

Bill Clinton Is A Wake-up Call

The Presidential Election of 1992 was a wake-up call to evangelical, Bible-believing Christians. In the course of the presidential debates, questions of character continually hounded Bill Clinton's bid for the White House. Accusations of marital infidelity threatened to derail the Clinton candidacy, as Jennifer Flowers leveled her charges of their long-running affair while Mr. Clinton was Governor of Arkansas. This incident resulted in the now famous Barbara Walters' interview of Bill and Hillary Clinton which aired their marital difficulties to a national audience. In the ensuing days we were told, "It's the economy, stupid!" "Character doesn't count," and "Foreign policy expertise is not necessary. What matters is a strong and vibrant economy." "I still believe in hope," the Hope, Arkansas, native told adoring audiences coast to coast.

Unlike the former presidential candidate, Gary Hart, whose campaign was abruptly terminated for moral indiscretions, Clinton survived the character issue and continued the campaign. Meanwhile, President George Bush and Vice President Dan Quayle were reviled for addressing family values. Dan Quayle's speech attacking Hollywood's glorification of single parenting, citing Murphy Brown, drew ridicule and scorn from a coalition of media, Hollywood and political liberals. As the specter of the elections loomed ahead, supporters of the Bush-Quayle ticket were overshadowed by sinister forces which diverted the focus from Clinton's moral character issues to platitudes of national concerns perceived to be "matters of substance." On election night Bill Clinton became the 42nd

President of the United States, although he received only forty-three percent of the popular vote.

The Radical Moral Agenda

Dr. James Dobson, heard on radio stations across America, reported in a publication dated January, 1994, that President Bill Clinton began the implementation of a radical moral agenda as soon as he was elected. Dr. Dobson offered the following overview of the first twelve months of the Clinton Presidency starting even before he was officially sworn in. Twelve days before Bill Clinton took office, the stage was set for what was coming. He received a letter signed by fifty-one members of Congress, including Patricia Schroeder and self-identified homosexuals Barney Frank and Gerry Studds, that contained the following paragraph:

> We are writing to express our support for an executive order prohibiting the ban on lesbians and gay men serving in the armed forces as soon as possible upon taking office in January. We will stand with you as you execute this historic executive order and will work with you to oppose any attempts to legislate this type of discrimination in the future.

On January 23, the third day of his administration, President Clinton remembered their request and did he ever deliver. He issued five executive orders that defined his agenda for leading our nation. They were designed to:

1. Lift the ban on homosexuals in the military, thus further legitimizing a life-style of destructive behavior that the Bible forbids.

2. Lift the ban on fetal tissue research that legalized treating preborn babies as if they were nothing more than laboratory mice.

3. Lift the ban on counseling in federally funded abortion clinics.

4. Begin the process of approving the importation of the abortion-inducing medication, RU486, ignoring the growing medical evidence of potential dangerous side effects, while making it

easier to slaughter innocent unborn children.

5. Provide funds, for the first time in history, for abortions in military hospitals.

During the next twelve months of Bill Clinton's Presidency, with lightening speed, the most radical anti-Christian social agenda in American history was implemented. Since the conservative resurgence of November 1994, he has been attempting to redefine himself as a "New Democrat," posturing himself as a moderate, but let us not forget that actions speak louder than words. Look at the record following January twenty-third and determine if it reflects the values that the majority of Americans hold dear.

- **February 3:** The Clinton Administration nominated Roberta Achtenberg for a prominent position in the Department of Housing and Urban Development. As an avowed lesbian activist, she spearheaded an attack on the Boy Scouts in San Francisco because they promoted values that, as she put it, "provides character building exclusively for straight, God-fearing male children."

- **February 11:** The Clinton Administration attempted to lift the restriction on the immigration of HIV-positive individuals into the United States. Fortunately, not even the Congress, dominated at the time by his own party, could support this move.

- **April 2:** Mr. Clinton initiated an attempt to repeal the Hyde Amendment which prohibits federal funding of abortions. Again, the Democratic controlled Congress rejected the proposal.

- **April 24:** An estimated 300,000 homosexual and lesbian activists descended on Washington, D.C., to celebrate America's first president sympathetic to their agenda. They chanted "Viva" (female genitalia) and "We're dykes, we're out, we're out for power!" (More will be said about such parades in chapter fourteen which is devoted to the homosexual movement in America.)

- **April 26:** Mr. Clinton's nominee for U.S. Surgeon General, Dr. Joycelyn Elders, announced, "I tell every girl that when she goes out on a date to put a condom in her purse."

- **April 28:** 217 years of military tradition was abandoned, as well as any opportunity for Congressional discussion, as the ban on women in combat was discarded by the Clinton White House. The implications for families and particularly children during wartime is incomprehensible.

- **June 10:** Mr. Clinton signed into law a bill lifting the restriction on fetal tissue research.

- **June 14:** Mr. Clinton appointed avowed feminist and ACLU activist, Ruth Bader Ginsberg to be an Associate Justice on the Supreme Court. She has taken controversial positions in the past which has included advocating the elimination of the traditional family in which the husband is the breadwinner and the wife is the homemaker. Endorsing her feminist positions, she has pursued the lowering of the age of consent for sexual acts to twelve years of age and she favors legalization of prostitution. She has also advocated elimination of all sex discrimination in the Boy Scouts and Girl Scouts, including a forced name change.

- **June 19:** Mr. Clinton sent a letter to Jon Larimore of the Gay and Lesbian Information Bureau thanking his organization for "selflessly giving their time and support to my administration..." "all of you who joined our ranks are making a real contribution to the future of our nation."

- **June 26:** Mr. Clinton appointed avowed lesbian Kristine Gebbie as the new AIDS czar. Four months later she said, "(The United States) needs to view human sexuality as an essentially important and pleasurable thing. (Until it does so) we will continue to be a repressed, Victorian society that misrepresents information, denies sexuality early, denies homosexual sexuality, particularly in teens, and leaves people abandoned with no place to go. I can help just a little bit on my job, standing on the White House lawn talking about sex with no lightning bolts falling on my head."

  (Author's note: It's interesting to note that she related the absence of lightning bolts as the apparent escape from divine displeasure, but never considered the plague of AIDS as a possibility.)

The above list represents the most radical social swing away from traditional Judeo-Christian morality in American history. An equal concern, however, was that the cascading sequence of events were all accomplished in the first six months of an administration that 57% of the American voting public rejected. Unfortunately, he was just getting started. Many agencies of the federal government were being targeted for liberalization.

Specific examples include the military, the National Endowment for the Arts, and the office of the Surgeon General.

- **July 29:** The Clinton White House announced the "Don't Ask, Don't Tell" policy regarding gays in the military.

- **August 5-6:** Congress passed the president's budget by one vote in the Senate, imposing one of the largest tax increases in American history, after campaigning on a pledge to cut taxes.

- **August 27:** The National Endowment for the Arts funded three gay and lesbian film festivals. The Executive Director of the Gay and Lesbian Media Coalition called the funding "...validation from the highest office for arts funding in the country."

- **September 4:** Plans were announced to invest up to seven billion dollars to reach ten to nineteen-year-olds with the failed message of condoms and safe sex.

- **September 4:** The Clinton White House diverted monies earmarked for Abstinence Based Sex-Ed curriculums into "safe sex" programs promoting condoms.

- **September 8:** Dr. Joycelyn Elders was confirmed as the new U.S. Surgeon General. She held the most radical views of any person to ever hold that office. After two years, even the Clinton Administration could no longer publicly embrace her outrageous statements and she was dismissed.

- **September 22:** Hillary Clinton began crusading for a National Health Care program.

- **September 23:** Mr. Clinton's Attorney General Janet Reno, under a brief filed before the Supreme Court that redefined child pornography, disclosed her view that producers and distributors of such ungodly material could not be prosecuted unless children were explicitly shown to be engaged in sexual conduct exposing the genitals or pubic area of the body.

- **October 9:** Mr. Clinton blasted the Religious Right for the first time, during a speech to Yale University.

- **October 18:** Mr. Clinton invited 12 evangelical leaders to a meeting at the White House. In the days that followed, sermons were preached and letters were written condemning Christians who had been critical of the President's policies.

- **November 2:** Homosexual and lesbian appointees in the Clinton Administration held a "coming out" breakfast for the press. They announced that twenty-two had been appointed, surpassing their goal of five. They applauded President Bill Clinton for his courage.

- **November 18:** The Clinton White House granted 13.2 million dollars to Planned Parenthood for overseas "family planning," today's trendy euphemism for killing unborn babies.

- **December 3:** In an interview with Tom Brokaw, Mr. Clinton expressed agreement with Dan Quayle's, Murphy Brown speech (Incomprehensible).

- **December 7:** The Clinton Administration announced a new ad campaign to provide explicit information on how to put on a condom.

- **December 7:** Joycelyn Elders announced that legalizing drugs would markedly reduce crime.

- **December 8:** The Clinton Administration added "sexual orientation" as a part of the revised nondiscrimination policies of the White House and key departments of government.

- **December 24:** Mr. Clinton announced he would require states to finance abortions for poor women who were made pregnant through rape or incest. (What a birthday present for the Savior of mankind!)

When I first received Dr. Dobson's mailout detailing the above summary of Mr. Clinton's first year of office, I could not believe my eyes. I filed away the information and tried to convince myself it was just an aberration and that Mr. Clinton would surely moderate his views. Unfortunately, the actions of 1993 were simply the harbingers of things to come. In 1994, more Christians registered to vote and went to the polls than any time in recent history. The results of the election sent shock waves throughout Washington and the liberal mainstream media.

Since January, 1995, the conservative majority in the Congress has been valiantly attempting to rollback many of the radical policies implemented by the Clinton Administration. Many of the new Congressmen elected in 1994 are committed Christians who ran for office in an effort to turn America back to Christ. They are dependent upon our prayers and our support.

The election of 1994 should encourage the heart of every true believer in Christ. The battle for America is not over. God has not yet abandoned us. But the hour is late. Winston Churchill, inspired Great Britain and her allies with his courage and oratory during World War II. After Great Britain defeated the German Army for their first victory of the war at the Battle of El Alamain in Africa, Churchill addressed the nation. He declared:

It is not the end, nor the beginning of the end. But it is perhaps the end of the beginning.

"The fundamental basis of this Nation's laws was given to Moses on the Mount...I don't think we emphasize that enough these days. If we don't have proper fundamental moral background, we will finally end up with a totalitarian government which does not believe in rights for anybody except the state."

-President Harry S. Truman

Chapter Two

Life In The
Fifties Was Good

My maternal grandfather and my dad spent their entire working lives employed at the local steel mill. In 1942, my grandfather, Marvin Campbell, transferred from Ashland, Kentucky, to Houston, Texas, to help open the Houston Division of Sheffield Steel. At age 16, my dad, Billy Jack Scarborough, moved from the farm in Kirvin, Texas, 175 miles north of Houston, and took a job in the steel mill. My grandfather left the mill in 1957 with terminal lung cancer. In 1982, the mill was closed. My father received an early retirement after spending thirty-seven years at the plant. In 1968, I worked at Sheffield for three months. My three months in the mold foundry was a lesson that has lasted a lifetime about real work. I am grateful to God for allowing me to see the price my father paid for thirty-seven years so that his family could enjoy a measure of the "good life." During those three months I worked in the steel mill, I decided that God had called me to go to college.

"Life In The Fifties Was Good." I was born on March 8, 1950, at the height of the postwar boom in America. After two devastating world wars, The Korean Conflict and the Great Depression which remained fresh in the mind of my father's generation, America entered a period of growth and prosperity.

What I Remember And Don't Remember

I remember living in a home without air conditioning, with only one black and white television, a rotary phone on a party line, and a chain link fence around the yard. At night, as the attic fan drew in the warm outside air, I would lie in my bedroom by the open window and smell the foul and familiar odor of the Pasadena Paper Mill. I remember hearing the pounding noises of the steel mill, over five miles away, as men labored around-the-clock.

I do not remember being afraid while living in a home where the only thing that protected me from the outside world was a thin screen on my open window. I do not remember my parents ever frantically searching our home for the car keys, because we always left them in the ignition of our car. I do not remember even locking the doors when we left our home, because in the 1950s, no one would dare invade the privacy of another person's home.

I do not remember ever seeing a child's photograph on the back of a milk carton or my mom telling me about the potential of being kidnapped or molested by a stranger. America was a great place to grow up in the fifties. I found out later that we were not affluent. While I was growing up, it sure did not bother me. I had a faithful father who always provided what we needed, a loving mother who never seemed to mind the monotonous labor that I now know it takes to keep up with the laundry, prepare all the meals, pack the lunches, and taxi everyone to school, ball practice, and piano lessons. As far as I could tell, it couldn't get much better.

"Life In The Fifties Was Good." I still love to watch old episodes of "Leave It To Beaver," "Father Knows Best" and "Ozzie and Harriet," because they bring back fond memories of life in America before the cultural revolution of the '60s.

During the post war boom, church played a central role for most Americans. Many main line denominations experienced great growth in the '50s. Southern Baptists put forth a campaign to recruit 1,000,000 new members in 1954... "A Million More in 54," the slogan urged.

I grew up in and around Galena Park, Texas, a suburb on the east side of Houston. Galena Park is adjacent to the Houston ship channel. I can remember going down to the docks as a little boy and being fascinated by the ships and seamen. My mother saw to it that my sister and I were always in church. Jacinto City is a small community adjacent to Galena Park. We moved into a neighborhood called Jacinto Oaks and attended Second Baptist Church in Jacinto City.

As a child, I loved going to church. I vividly remember the evening I committed my life to Jesus Christ. As a seven-year-old, I was all boy. I have often told groups that I had a unique calling on my life as a seven year old child. My dad did not go to church, so I felt a margin of freedom to "do my own thing" while there. I knew I could handle Mom. Though the men of the church might have wanted to whip me, I knew they wouldn't. As a result of this freedom, I developed a new ministry. My ministry was sifting out all the teachers who weren't truly called to teach children. After a few weeks with me in their class, teachers would reexamine their ministry. They would either renew their commitment to teach children or quit.

When Second Baptist Church completely remodeled their sanctuary in 1973, no one was more grateful than I. Why? Because they removed an old theater-style seat from the back row of the church where, during a morning worship service about fifteen years earlier, I carved my name in the armrest...with my teeth. That's right, my teeth. Alan, my childhood friend and coconspirator in numerous other like-endeavors, joined me as we got down on our knees and used the preaching time to carve our names. I got the whipping of my life for the stunt, but the reminder of my sin remained on that armrest to haunt me for years to come. The people of Second Baptist Church loved to take their friends by my memorial chair every time I preached over the ensuing years.

I Gave My Heart To Jesus

Though I was almost always pulling some dumb stunt, I truly loved the church. Marie Smith was my Sunday School teacher in the seven-year-old department. During our Sunday School lesson one Sunday morning, she discerned that God was dealing in my heart. She perceptively scheduled to visit me in my home the next evening. I will never forget that experience on that Monday night as she walked me through John 3:16:

"For God so loved the world that he gave his only begotten Son, that whosoever believeth in him should not perish but have everlasting life" (KJV).

She explained the gospel to me in meaningful terms. She explained that I could insert my name in the verse in the place of "the world" and that the "whosoever" included me. When she concluded her remarks, I gave my heart to Jesus. The following Sunday morning, she stood by my side as I quoted John 3:16, the first verse I remember memorizing. I also quoted the first verse of that great old hymn, "He Lives:"

I serve a risen Savior, He's in the world today;

I know that He is living, whatever men may say;
I see His hand of mercy, I hear His voice of cheer,
And just the time I need Him, He's always near.
He lives, He lives, Christ Jesus lives today!
He walks with me and talks with me along life's narrow way.
He lives, He lives, salvation to impart!
You ask me how I know He lives: He lives within my heart."

We Had Connecting Points

There were many connecting points for my generation.

Stable Families: I knew of only one family in our entire neighborhood that went through divorce. I am sure there were others, but I knew of only one.

The Church: Little League would not think of scheduling a ball game on Wednesday night because it was prayer meeting night.

The Schools: Public Schools were an extension of our homes. They taught the same values we were taught at home and demanded responsible behavior.

The Neighborhood: I had no doubt that Alan's, John's, Glen's, Robert's or Donnie's parents all expected the same behavior out of me as did my own parents. At various times each of those fellows was my best friend and at all times, we were all pals. We started grade one together and we graduated from grade twelve together. There was not a broken home or a family that relocated in the entire group. My, how times have changed.

But that was then. This is now. How could we go from a society where divorce was almost nonexistent, the church was the center of the community, the school's greatest discipline problems were talking and chewing gum, and neighborhoods seldom witnessed "for sale" signs; to a society where divorce has become the rule, church is considered irrelevant, schools are installing metal detectors and the average family moves twelve times, in only forty years?

Not only do I believe the answers are found in God's Word, but I believe our current state of affairs was clearly predicted in Scripture. I intend to show in the following pages that the only hope for this nation is a national revival. I am calling you, the reader, to do two things. Please look at the truth with an open mind, and then ask God to give you the courage to do something about what you read. This book is a call to action. You will read some discouraging information, but in the end, this book is a book of hope containing concrete instructions on how we can restore America to her Christian heritage. The words of II Chronicles 7:14 should ever ring in our hearts:

"If my people, who are called by my name, will humble themselves and pray and seek my face and turn from their wicked ways, then will I hear from heaven and will forgive their sin and will heal their land."

William Bennett writes these important thoughts in the preface of his important work, *The Devaluing of America:*

The American people have overcome enormous challenges before. And I have seen, and much of this book recounts, the difference that good, decent and courageous men and women can make. Our cultural injuries are self-inflicted. The good news is that what has been self-inflicted can be self-corrected.

"The highest glory of the American Revolution was this, it connected in one indissoluble bond, principles of civil government with the principles of Christianity."

-John Quincy Adams - July 4, 1821

Chapter Three

America Was Established On Christian Principles

Peter Marshall and David Manual have made a valuable contribution to our nation. In their two volumes, *The Light and The Glory* and its sequel, *From Sea to Shining Sea,* they trace the clear role that faith in Christ has played in the founding, shaping, and sustaining of this great nation. They reveal the true heart of Christopher Columbus, who recorded in his diary his driving conviction that his purpose in life was to take the good news of Jesus Christ to the heathen of the Far East. It was not an accident that Columbus chose to name his first discovered island, San Salvador... which means Holy Savior. God's guidance in the founding of America is unmistakable.

I would not be so foolish as to assert that it was only Christians who first came to America or that all of their motives were pure. However, it is clear that many who shaped the formation of this nation were committed to Jesus Christ and held a firm belief that God was doing something unique and very grand.

In 1609, because of persecution for their religious beliefs, a group of Christians, later known as Pilgrims, left their homes and families in Scrooby, England, and fled to the Netherlands. There they found some religious tolerance. They settled in Leyden, Holland, and formed the English Separatist church.

In 1620, they became concerned that their children were losing their English identity and they were still thwarted in their efforts to worship God as they chose. These Pilgrims decided to go to the New World where they could live as Englishmen and have the freedom to worship as they saw fit. Unable to finance the trip, they indentured themselves for seven years to a group of English businessmen. Prior to leaving in September of 1620, their pastor, Rev. John Robinson, called them to a solemn fast and then delivered a sermon in which he said:

> I charge you, before God and his blessed angels, that you follow me no further than you have seen me follow the Lord Jesus Christ. The Lord has more truth yet to break forth out of his Holy Word. I cannot sufficiently bewail the condition of the reformed churches, who are come to a period in religion, and will go at present no further than the instruments of their reformation. - Luther and Calvin were great and shinning lights in their times, yet they penetrated not into the whole counsel of God. - I beseech you, remember it, - 'tis an article of your church covenant, - that you be ready to receive whatever truth shall be made known to you from the written word of God.

For sixty-six days, the Mayflower pitched and rolled as stormy seas continually battered the ship. Marshall and Manuel recount how that in the hold, that grew increasingly foul with each passing day, were 102 weary and pitiful passengers that would be responsible for carrying out the initial settlement of a new nation that one day would be known around the world as the "land of the free and the home of the brave."

The Pilgrims landed on the tip of Cape Cod on November 21, 1620. They then sailed on to Plymouth where, in late December, they established a permanent settlement. Plymouth was a religious colony governed by biblical standards. William Bradford, who served as their second governor and the colonial historian, wrote in his *History of Plymouth Plantation, Book I:*

> Last and not least, they cherished a great hope and inward zeal of laying good foundations, or at least of making some way towards it, for the propagation and advance of the gospel of the kingdom of Christ in the remote parts of the world, even though they should be but stepping stones to others in the performance of so great a work.

These first settlers were on a mission from God. Because of their deep and unwavering love for, and commitment to Him and to His purpose in their lives, they were willing to endure whatever sacrifice was required, and without complaining. They pressed on, surviving the voyage and arriving in the new world to serve as indentured servants on the Plymouth Plantation. As Marshall and Manuel point out, they were ordinary Christian families about to establish an extraordinary Christian nation called America.

The Mayflower Compact, gives irrefutable evidence that Jesus was Lord of those first Pilgrims and that they understood their purpose in coming to America. Facing many overwhelming obstacles and dangers, they pledged:

> In the name of God, Amen. We whose names are underwritten, the loyal subjects of our dread Sovereign Lord King James by the grace of God of Great Britain, France, Ireland, King, Defender of the Faith, etc.
>
> Having undertaken, for the glory of God and the advancement of the Christian faith and honor of our King and country, a voyage to plant the first colony in the northern parts of Virginia, do by these presents solemnly and mutually in the presence of God and one of another, covenant and combine ourselves together and a civil body politic.

America's first political document reflected the desire of its signers to glorify God and to advance the Christian faith.

The Reformation And Its Effects

When one sets out to discover truth from history, it is vitally important to remember these past events, even as those of today, always take place in a context. The Reformation had taken Europe out of the dark ages and revolutionized not only the church, but governments as well. For the first time, everything was evaluated in the light of the Scripture, which was available to the people.

True freedom became a tangible possibility, as man realized he was accountable to God. For the first time, common people could understand the biblical principle of their own sin nature, and with God's help, learn to restrain their behavior. John Whitehead observes of the Reformation and its effects:

> Freedom could exist without chaos. The event led to a culture that brought about civil freedoms and benefits Western Europe

and the United States have enjoyed for centuries.

Christian theism teaches that man is held accountable to his Creator. Absolute standards exist by which all moral judgments of life are to be measured. With the Bible, there is a standard of right and wrong.

The Law and The Prince

During the medieval period, the doctrine of the Divine Right of Kings, which asserted that the king was above the law and was exempt from its jurisdiction, led to tragic abuses of power. Rev. Samuel Rutherford, a Presbyterian minister, published a book in 1644 entitled *Lex Rex* or *The Law And The Prince*. *Lex Rex* asserted that the premise of all law must be biblically-based. He proposed God's Holy Word was the foundation of truth and all men, including the king were under the law. Rutherford's ideas had great influence on subsequent generations.

One of those greatly impacted by the writings of Rev. Samuel Rutherford was the Rev. John Witherspoon, a Presbyterian minister who was educated at the Edinburgh University. Rev. Witherspoon was the only clergyman to sign the Declaration of Independence, and he brought the principles of *Lex Rex* into the formation of the Constitution. Rev. Witherspoon was a central player in preparing the Judeo-Christian foundation of America as president and chief lecturer at the College of New Jersey (later named Princeton) from 1768-1793. He touched the lives of nearly 500 graduates. Eleven percent of them became presidents of colleges. James Madison, known as the father of the Constitution, was his most notable student.

Witherspoon taught a vice president, twenty-one senators, thirty-nine representatives, fifty-six state legislators and thirty-three judges, three of whom became members of the United States Supreme Court. [1]

As the building blocks of America were being laid, the founding fathers were determined that her government would be built on Christian principles. Francis Schaeffer observed that many...

> of the men who laid the foundation of the United States Constitution were not Christians in the full sense, and yet they built upon the basis of the Reformation, either directly through the *Lex Rex* tradition or indirectly through (John) Locke. [2]

Early settlers were unashamed of Christ. We have been besieged with misinformation over the past thirty years that has caused many in our country to believe America was never a Christian nation. Children in today's sterile, secular, educational environment are being led to believe that God had nothing to do with the formulation of America and our founders never intended for religion to be discussed in the public arena. That is a lie and an insult to the truth of our history. Consider:

> The first colony successfully established in America was the Jamestown Colony in 1607. The first Charter of Virginia stated: "We, greatly commending and graciously accepting of, their desires for the furtherance of so noble a work, which may, by the providence of Almighty God, hereafter tend to the glory of His Divine Majesty, in propagating of the Christian religion to such people, as yet live in darkness and miserable ignorance of the true knowledge and worship of God, and may in time bring the infidels and savages living in those parts to human civility and to a settled and quiet government, do, by these our letters patent, graciously accept of, and agree to, their humble and well-intended desires." [3]

On 1620, as previously discussed, the Pilgrims established Plymouth Plantation. In 1638, the Rev. John Davenport assisted Theophilus Eaton in establishing New Haven, Connecticut. That same year the first general court met and enacted a body of laws for the colony based entirely on the Word of God. In 1659, a committee consisting of seven, known as the "Seven Pillars," were appointed to enact a "civil polity where God's Word was established as the only rule in public affairs." [4] The Bible became the Statute Book for Connecticut. The seven included Rev. Davenport, who was their pastor, and Eaton, who had become their governor, an office which he served in for twenty years.

In January 14, 1639, the Fundamental Orders of Connecticut, known as the world's first written constitution, was adopted by the colonists. The following phrases from the document reveal what those colonists believed about the relationship between religion and the State:

> Forasmuch as it has pleased Almighty God by the wise disposition of His Divine Providence so to order and dispose of things that we the inhabitants and residents of Windsor, Hartford and Wethersfield, and now cohabiting and dwelling in and upon the river Conectecotte [Connecticut] and the lands thereunto adjoining; and well knowing where a people are gathered together

the Word of God requires that to maintain the peace and union of such a people there should be an orderly and decent government established according to God, to order and dispose of the affairs of all the people at all seasons as occasions shall require; do therefore associate and conjoin ourselves to be as one public State or Commonwealth, and do, for ourselves and our successors and such as shall be adjoined to us at any time hereafter, enter into combination and confederation together, to maintain and preserve the liberty and purity of the Gospel of our Lord Jesus which we now profess, as also the discipline of the churches, which according to the truth of the said Gospel is now practiced among us. [5]

As you read these early documents, it becomes clear that these early settlers were committed to being a pleasure to God. God, in turn, was committed to their success. On May 19, 1643, the Articles of Confederation between Massachusetts, New Plymouth, Connecticut and New Haven, were enacted. They were known as the New England Confederation. One phrase in the Articles sums up the purpose and intent of the early settlers...

Whereas we all came into these parts of America with one and the same end and aim, namely, to advance the Kingdom of our Lord Jesus Christ...[6]

In 1665, the colonial legislature of New York, which was under the supervision of England, passed a law ordering the people of every parish to build a church large enough to hold 200 persons. The minister was instructed to preach every Sunday and to pray for the king, queen, Duke of York and the royal family.

The preamble to a body of laws enacted in 1695 says much about how the early settlers felt about whether or not Christianity should be separated from state policies:

Whereas, the true and sincere worship of God, according to His holy will and commandments, is often profaned and neglected by many of the inhabitants and sojourners in this Province who do not keep holy the Lord's day, but in a disorderly manner accustom themselves to travel, laboring, working, shooting, fishing, sporting, playing, horse racing, frequenting tippling-houses, and the using of many other unlawful exercises and pastimes, upon the Lord's day, to the great scandal of the holy Christian faith...[7]

State Constitutions Reflect A Christian Commitment

A survey of the State Constitutions that preceded the Revolutionary War reflects the same consecration toward America being a Christian nation. The evidence in the historical record is simply overwhelming.

The Delaware Constitution of 1776 required all office seekers to hold certain theological convictions:

> Article 22. Every person who shall be chosen a member of either house, or appointed to any office or place of trust...shall...also make and subscribe the following declaration to wit: "I, _____, do profess faith in God the Father, and in Jesus Christ His only Son, and in the Holy Ghost, one God, blessed for evermore, and I do acknowledge the holy scriptures of the Old and New Testament to be given by divine inspiration." [8]

The New Jersey Constitution of 1771 stipulated that "no person shall ever...be deprived of the inestimable privilege of worshipping Almighty God in a manner agreeable to the dictates of his own conscience." These are not the sterile words of a deist or humanist, but rather of someone who has had a genuine understanding of the nature of a true worship experience.

The Maryland Constitution reflects a deep commitment to protecting orthodox Christianity, even though Maryland, unlike the other Protestant colonies, was founded by Catholics. Article XXXIII states:

> All persons, professing the Christian religion, are equally entitled to protection in their religious liberty; wherefore no person ought by any law to be molested in his person or estate on account of his religious persuasion or profession, or for this religious practice; unless, under colour of religion, any man shall disturb the good order, peace and safety of the State. [9]

Though the colony was established by Catholics, their history of religious intolerance in the Old World caused them to safeguard, in their laws, against such abuse.

Pennsylvania was founded by William Penn. In 1682, he cited I Timothy 1:9-10 as the biblical basis for civil government. Referencing Romans 13:1-5 he stated, "This settles the divine right of government beyond exception, and that for two ends. First, to terrify evil doers; secondly, to cherish those who do well."[10]

The earliest official documents of Pennsylvania perpetually required her office holders to swear by oath some form of commitment to Jesus Christ. In a 1705-06 act of the legislature, civil magistrates were required to...

> profess to believe in Jesus Christ, the Savior of the world and swear that they profess faith in God the Father and in Jesus Christ his eternal Son, the true God, and in the Holy Spirit, one God blessed for evermore; and do acknowledge the Holy Scriptures of the Old Testament and New Testament to be given by divine inspiration.[11]

On June 16, 1775, the Provincial Congress passed a resolution acknowledging the sin of failing to keep the Lord's Day holy. There was no fear of allowing their religion to encroach upon their civil duties in that generation.

> And whereas there is great danger that the profanation of the Lord's Day will prevail in the camp: We earnestly recommend to all the officers, not only to set good examples; but that they strictly require of their soldiers to keep up a religious regard to that Day, and attend public worship of God thereon, so far as may be consistent with other duties.[12]

An Important Reminder

The United States of America was originally comprised of thirteen, very independent colonies, each founded by men and women who were fleeing oppressive and restrictive regimes in Europe. They bonded together to throw off that oppressive yoke. Today's secularists would have us believe that our founding fathers intended to keep religion and public policy separate. Reading their writings and quotes reveals the magnitude of the lie perpetrated on the American people during the last thirty years. I am a strong proponent of the philosophy that says "You don't refute error with silence. You refute error with truth." Jesus said, "Ye shall know the truth and the truth shall set you free." God is looking for courageous men who will stare down the infidels and uphold the truth, and the truth is: America was founded as a Christian nation. Our forefathers sacrificed their lives and fortunes to carve out "One Nation Under God." In one generation of silent neglect, we have allowed the revisionists of our history to rewrite our past and deny that we have a Christian heritage. In truth, the proof of our Christian heritage is overwhelming.

America Was Established By Men Committed To Christ

Secularists do not understand the nature of Christianity. Unlike other religious systems, Christianity is a relationship with God. It has been accurately described as "Christ-in-you-ity." When Christ comes into your heart, He then affects every area of your life. Where you go, He goes. What you do, He does. Therefore, if a Christian decides to serve in public office, in effect, Jesus, through his life, serves in public office. Hence, Christianity cannot be kept out of politics.

Our original founding fathers understood that very well. It was said of Simon Peter, as he stood by the campfire on the eve of the crucifixion, "thy speech betrayeth thee." (See Matthew 26:73) The speech of our founding fathers, likewise, reveals their commitment to building a nation on Christian principles.

John Peter Muhlenberg was my favorite colonial character. In 1774, he was both a member of the Virginia House of Burgesses and a pastor who regularly preached on Christian responsibility. His father, Henry Muhlenberg, was one of the founders of the Lutheran Church in America.

In 1775, after preaching on Ecclesiastes 3:1 which says: "For everything there is a season and a time for every matter under heaven," he closed with these words; "In the language of the Holy Writ, there is a time for all things. There is a time to preach and a time to fight." [13]

He then removed his robe to reveal a Revolutionary Army uniform and announced he was prepared to fight for the cause of freedom. Two hundred men followed him off to join General Washington who made him the Colonel of the Eighth Virginia Regiment. He served throughout the war and achieved the rank of Major General. After the war, he held numerous political offices, including being elected to the U.S. Senate in 1801.[14]

Ethan Allen, an American Revolutionary War hero and commander of the Green Mountain Boys, led his troops in a surprise attack on May 10, 1775. They surrounded Ft. Ticonderoga on Lake Champlain, where they demanded that the fort be surrendered instantaneously. When Captain de la Place asked in whose name and by what authority Commander Allen made such a demand, he responded, "In the name of the Great Jehovah and the Continental Congress." [15]

Samuel Chase was appointed to the Supreme Court by George Washington. He was also a signer of the Declaration of Independence. In 1799, Justice Chase, in the case of *Runkel v. Winsmiller*, wrote:

> By our form of Government, the Christian religion is the established religion; and all sects and denominations of Christians are placed on the same equal footing, and are equally entitled to protection in their religious liberty. [16]

I doubt very seriously if Justice Chase would have ruled to ban prayer and reading the Bible in the public schools or posting the Ten Commandments on the walls of a school building. Notice, he wrote "By our form of government, the Christian religion is the established religion."

In the Summer of 1787, representatives met in Philadelphia to write the Constitution of the United States of America. They struggled in confusion for weeks until the eighty-one year old Benjamin Franklin, whom we are often told was not a Christian, spoke these words:

> In the beginning of the Contest with G. Britain, when we were sensible of danger, we had daily prayers in this room for divine protection. Our prayers, Sir, were heard and they were graciously answered. All of us who were engaged in the struggle must have observed frequent instances of a superintending providence in our favor...Have we now forgotten this powerful Friend? Or do we imagine we no longer need His assistance? I have lived long, Sir, a long time, and the longer I live the more convincing proof I see of this truth: that God governs in the affairs of man. And if a sparrow cannot fall to the ground without his notice, is it probable that an empire can rise without His aid? We have been assured, Sir, in the Sacred Writings that except the Lord build the house, they labor in vain that build it. I firmly believe this...I therefore beg leave to move that, henceforth, prayers imploring

the assistance of Heaven and its blessing on our deliberation be held in this assembly every morning.[17]

I wish all the members of the church I pastor had such insight into God's truth. Rev. George Whitefield, whose preaching in the years preceding the American Revolution shook two continents and helped ignite the "Great Awakening" that swept through the colonies prior to the Revolutionary War, had a deep and abiding friendship with Benjamin Franklin. Whether or not Franklin was ever converted, God used His prophet to prepare the philosopher-politician for the important work He was about to perform in leading the formation of a new nation.

Speaking of the power and impact of Franklin's speech, Jonathan Dayton, stated:

> The Doctor sat down; and never did I behold a countenance at once so dignified and delighted as was that of Washington at the close of the address; nor were the members of the convention generally less affected. The words of the venerable Franklin fell upon our ears with a weight and authority, even greater that we may suppose an oracle to have had in a Roman senate![18]

Our founding fathers also knew that freedom could only exist if men chose to restrain themselves from within. Listen to their own words:

Francis Marion was a courageous Major General in the Revolutionary War. He was dubbed "old swamp fox," by British General Banastre Tarleton. Francis Marion stated, "In short, the religion of Jesus Christ is the only sure and controlling power over sin." [19]

John Adams was the second president of the United States. In an address to the military, delivered on October 11, 1798, he stated:

> We have no government armed with power capable of contending with human passions unbridled by morality and religion. Avarice, ambition, revenge, or gallantry, would break the strongest cords of our Constitution as a whale goes through a net. Our Constitution was made only for a moral and religious people. It is wholly inadequate to the government of any other.[20]

James Madison was known as the "Chief Architect" of our

Constitution. He became the fourth president of the United States. Before studying law, he prepared for the ministry and studied theology. He wrote:

> We have staked the whole future of American civilization, not upon the power of government, far from it. We have staked the future of all our political institutions upon the capacity of mankind for self-government; upon the capacity of each and all of us to govern ourselves, to control ourselves, to sustain ourselves, according to the Ten Commandments of God.[21]

John Jay was the first Chief Justice of the United States appointed by George Washington. He was also elected President of the American Bible Society in 1821. On October 12, 1816, he admonished:

> Providence has given to our people the choice of their rulers, and it is the duty as well as the privilege and interests of our Christian nation to select and prefer Christians for their rulers.[22]

Daniel Webster, who authored America's first Exhaustive Dictionary observed:

> Whatever makes men good Christians, makes them good citizens.[23]

Alexander Hamilton was not only a signer of the Constitution, he was known as the "ratifier of the Constitution." Of the Constitution, he stated:

> For my own part, I sincerely esteem it a system which without the finger of God, never could have been suggested and agreed upon by such a diversity of interests.[24]

In 1802, he suggested in a letter to a friend, organizing "'The Christian Constitutional Society,' its object to be first: the support of the Christian religion; second: the support of the United States." [25]

Hamilton wrote: "...natural liberty is a gift of the beneficent Creator, to the whole human race; and that civil liberty is founded in that; and cannot be wrested from any people, without the most manifest violation of justice." [26]

George Washington is known as the Father of America. The acknowledgments of his faith in Christ are enough to fill greater books than I am writing. His farewell address, given at the end of his presidency, is still one of the high points of oratory in our history. For years it was included in virtually every American history book. Not surprising, it has been omitted in recent years, perhaps because of its "offensive" religious content.

I believe the "Father of this Country," the "Commander in Chief" of the Continental Army and our first President would be a good authority to consult when considering the intent of our founding fathers regarding the role of religion in civil affairs and the affairs of our nation. His inaugural speech, given to both Houses of Congress on April 30, 1789, set the tone for his presidency:

> Such being the impressions under which I have, in obedience to the public summons, repaired to the present station, it would be peculiarly improper to omit, in this first official act, my fervent supplications to that Almighty Being who rules over the universe, who presides in the councils of nations and whose providential aids can supply every human defect, that His benediction may consecrate to the liberties and happiness of the people of the United States a Government instituted by themselves for these essential purposes; and may enable every instrument employed in its administration to execute with success, the functions allotted to his charge.
>
> In tendering this homage to the Great Author of every public and private good, I assure myself that it expresses your sentiments not less than my own; nor those of my fellow-citizens at large, less than either.
>
> No people can be bound to acknowledge and adore the Invisible Hand which conducts the affairs of men more than the people of the United States. Every step by which they have advanced to the character of an independent nation seems to have been distinguished by some token of providential agency; and in the important revolution just accomplished in the system of their united government, the tranquil deliberations and voluntary consent of so many distinct communities, from which the event has resulted cannot be compared with the means by which most governments have been established, without some return of pious gratitude, along with an humble anticipation of the future blessings which the past seem to presage. These

reflections, arising out of the present crisis, have forced themselves too strongly on my mind to be suppressed. You will join with me I trust in thinking, that there are none under the influence of which the proceedings of a new and free government can more auspiciously commence.

We ought to be no less persuaded that the propitious smiles of Heaven can never be expected on a nation that disregards the eternal rules of order and right which Heaven itself has ordained; and since the preservation of the sacred fire of liberty and the destiny of the republican model of government are justly considered as deeply, perhaps finally, staked of the experiment...

I shall take my present leave; but not without resorting once more to the Benign Parent of the Human Race, in humble supplication that, since He has been pleased to favor the American people with opportunities for deliberating in perfect tranquillity, and dispositions for deciding with unparalleled unanimity on a form of government for the security of their union and the advancement of their happiness, so His divine blessings may be equally conspicuous in the enlarged views, the temperate consultations and the wise measures on which the success of this Government must depend.[27]

In Washington's last address to the Congress, he made an impacting statement regarding his personal view of the role of the Bible and government. "It is impossible to rightly govern the world without God and the Bible..." "It is impossible to govern the universe without the aid of a Supreme Being." George Washington understood the importance of God's protection being placed around the nation: "Let us unite in imploring the Supreme Ruler of nations to spread his holy protection over these United States."

In Washington's Farewell Address to the nation, he made many remarkable observations:

The name of American, which belongs to you, in your national capacity, must always exalt the just pride of patriotism, more than any appellation derived from local discriminations. With slight shades of difference, you have same religion, manners, habits and political principles...Of all the dispositions and habits which led to political prosperity, religion and morality are indispensable supports.

In vain would that man claim the tribute of patriotism, who should labor to subvert these great pillars of human happiness, these firmest props of the duties of men and citizens. The new politician, equally with the pious man, ought to respect and to cherish them. A volume could not trace all their connections with private and public felicity. Let it simply be asked where is the security for prosperity, for reputation, for life, if the sense of religious obligation desert the oaths, which are the instruments of investigation in the courts of justice?

And let us with caution indulge the supposition, that morality can be maintained without religion. Whatever may be conceded to the influence of refined education on minds of peculiar structure, reason and experience both forbid us to expect that national morality can prevail in exclusion of religious principle. Tis substantially true, that virtue or morality is a necessary spring of popular government. ...Can it not be that Providence has not connected the permanent felicity of a nation with its virtue?"[28]

These insightful words spoken on September 19, 1796, were words of prophecy. For the better part of two centuries, this nation maintained a clear cultural identity. The name, "American," applied to a people who held the same religion, habits and political principles, with only shades of difference. How far we have fallen as a nation! When are we going to finally decide "Enough is Enough?"

"Our laws and our institutions must necessarily be based upon and embody the teachings of the Redeemer of mankind. It is impossible that it should be otherwise, and in this sense and to this extent our civilization and our institutions are emphatically Christian."

-Justice Josiah Brewer
United States Supreme Court,
Feb. 29, 1892
Church of the Holy Trinity
v. United States

Chapter Four

American Institutions Were Built On Biblical Truth

Christianity and biblical revelation enabled the framers of our nation to structure a governmental system unlike any the world had ever known. The United States of America is often referred to as a democracy, but the United States was designed to be a Constitutional Republic. The framers of our nation were very acquainted with the numerous biblical examples of the majority being wrong. When Moses came down from his forty days alone with God, bearing the Ten Commandments, he discovered that Aaron had facilitated the desires of the majority by building them a golden calf to worship. The majority was wrong. Their actions were corrected, not by a vote, but rather by the law.

That biblical revelation aided our founding fathers as they conceived our Constitutional Republic. Over the past forty years while the general public has been brainwashed to believe that majority means right, the liberals of our nation have targeted the courts to begin changing the meaning of our Constitution. Liberal judicial scholars have coined a new term to facilitate their assault on the Constitution. It is now referred to as a "living document." Justices, beginning with the "Everson" court in 1947, said the Constitution means whatever the majority on the court says it means. More will be mentioned of this important departure from the historical role of the courts in chapter six.

In America, today there is a growing rejection of all absolutes; hence, a "living," as opposed to "fixed" Constitution. This has resulted in a nation adrift in a sea of moral relativism. Ask any public school teacher to list for you the core values that hold the MTV generation of young people together. The only absolute that remains for many is the absolute right to "do what I want to do," whether that means stealing your Reeboks, raping your daughter, or driving by and shooting into your home.

The framers of our nation created the most prosperous country the world has ever witnessed. They designed a republic based on law that was derived from biblical revelation. The Declaration of Independence reflected their commitment to absolute truth:

> We hold these truths to be self-evident, that all men are created equal, that they are endowed by their Creator with certain unalienable rights, that among these are life, liberty, and the pursuit of happiness.

In the closing line of the Declaration of Independence, they refer to their willingness to risk their fortunes and their lives with the confidence that "Divine Providence" would assist them. In today's political climate, the American Civil Liberties Union would likely sue them for such overt religious language. But then again, such threats to personal property or liberty would not have intimidated the men who signed such a document. God is again looking for such men.

America: Designed To Be Governed By Three Branches
The framers of our nation understood the sin nature of man. This biblical revelation empowered them to create a model that the world would envy. Not only did they design a constitutional republic, but understanding the nature of mankind and his propensity toward corruption, they designed a threefold "checks and balances" system. Having been the recipients of the tyrannical rule of monarchs, they distributed the power to govern among three branches of government. The wisdom of this strategy prevented a popular president from setting up a kingdom. When a president abuses his power, he is checked by the legislative and/ or the judicial branches. When the legislature begins to garner too much power, or enact laws that are burdensome or unwholesome, they are checked by the executive and/or judicial branches. And when the courts begin to abuse their power, they are checked by the executive and/or the legislative branches.

This system worked flawlessly until the judicial branch happened upon the trendy "living constitution" theory that now dominates discussion among many in our law schools.

America: Designed To Be Prospered By Free Enterprise

The framers of our nation also devised a new economic order, again reflecting their biblical understanding of sinful human nature, known as the Free Enterprise System. The Free Enterprise System in its purist form rewards hard work and punishes sloth. II Thessalonians 3:10 presents the underlying principle of Free Enterprise Capitalism: "For even when we were upon you, we gave you this rule: 'If a man will not work, he shall not eat.'"

In the Plymouth Plantation Colony, after experimenting with a form of socialism the first year, William Bradford enforced this precept. Recognizing that among the settlers were a number of lazy sluggards whose sloth was endangering them all, he made drastic changes in the operation of the colony. When it became evident that his Christian benevolence did not extend to include excusing laziness, everyone pitched in and worked the fields. II Thessalonians 3:10 was the underlying principle that prompted the changes.

The Parable of the Talents, given by Jesus, and recorded in Matthew 25:14-28 teaches a principle understood by the founding fathers that is unimaginable in the minds of today's economic socialists and their bankrupt theories of redistribution. In the parable, a man going on a journey calls his three servants to a meeting, announces his intentions, and then entrusts shares of his property to each of them to oversee during his absence. To one he gives five talents, to another he grants two, and to a third he grants only one.

The two servants who have received five and two talents, respectively, decide to take risks and invest their master's money. When he returns he discovers that each have doubled their talents and are able to give to their master a one-hundred percent return. His response is equally full of praise to the one who returns four as to the one who returns ten. They are declared good and faithful, and promised greater rewards. The third servant who only has one talent, decides not to take any risks. He instead simply buries the talent, failing even to take advantage of a risk-free savings account drawing the master an interest payment.

It is important to note that at least this servant did not waste the money by spending it on selfish pursuits, yet the response of the master is to condemn the servant harshly and take the one talent away. While the "worthless" servant was carried away, the talent was given to the man with ten. What was the third servant guilty of doing that merited the description of "worthless?" The sin of idleness, doing nothing. The master rewarded the industrious servant with still another talent while condemning the idle servant to be tormented.

Our founding fathers knew that God rewards hard work and risk taking. They also understood that every man is lazy at his core and if laziness is ever rewarded it will soon destroy any economic system, regardless of how sound it may appear.

Today's economic socialists would see this third servant as being deprived in that he only had one talent. They would rule that the man who had ten had too many (too much wealth). They would then punish him for being successful by taking away five talents and giving four to the man who had one and giving one to the man who had four, so all would have five. Then they would likely tax all three at an exorbitant rate to pay their overhead expenses for being "so caring." Meanwhile, the ambition and drive to succeed would be destroyed.

America: Designed To Be Wise

Our founding fathers created a new method of governance and a new economic system, both reflecting their biblical values, but they did so much more than that. They worked diligently to build a strong and productive educational system as well. They believed that whoever controlled the educational system, controlled the future agenda of the nation. The Reformation had taught them how important education was in effecting the advancement of Christian civilization.

In 1690, the first edition of the *New England Primer* appeared. It gained wide acceptance by 1700. It was developed by Benjamin Harris and included an ingenious way to learn the alphabet. He included in it basic biblical truths and lessons about life. Students would chant, in unison:

A   In Adam's fall, we sinned all,
B   Thy life to mend, this Book attend,
C   The Cat doth play, and after slay,

In 1777, the Primer was enlarged to include even more biblical material. For instance, that edition included:

C   For sinners died, Christ crucified

The founding fathers started a number of colleges and universities between 1636 and 1769, and all but one were distinctly Christian. [29]

Date	College	Colony	Affiliation
1636	Harvard	Massachusetts	Puritan
1693	William and Mary	Virginia	Anglican
1701	Yale	Connecticut	Congregational
1746	Princeton	New Jersey	Presbyterian
1754	King's College	New York	Anglican
1764	Brown	Rhode Island	Baptist
1766	Rutgers	New Jersey	DutchReformed
1769	Dartmouth	New Hampshire	Congregational

The primary purpose of these schools was to train men for the gospel ministry, but their curriculum was very comprehensive. Churches expected their ministers to be able to read the Scriptures in the original languages.

Today, many are shocked to discover that most of the nation's Ivy League schools were founded by Christians, and used to hold to the belief that the Scripture is the foundation of all truth. The early motto of Harvard was *Vertas Christo et Ecclesia* (Truth of Christ and the Church). Harvard's founders believed that truth was discovered in Christ and His Word. Ari Goldman, in his book, *The Search for God at Harvard* writes:

> Religion was so much a part of every day learning in the early days of Harvard that for nearly two centuries no one thought of setting up a separate Divinity School. In college, the students gathered daily for prayer and readings from the Scripture. Hebrew as well as Greek were required subjects, because an educated person was expected to be able to read the Bible in the original tongues. [30]

Today, Christians who are speaking out about their faith are often branded as religious extremists who want to assert their morality on others. Bashing the Religious Right has become acceptable political sport. The truth is, what many of the Christian Right are demanding is that America simply return to the clear intent of those who purchased our freedom with their blood. They are saying, "Enough is Enough."

The fact that America was established as a Christian nation is without question when the historical record is allowed to speak. As the founding fathers sought to honor God as they built their new nation, He in turn provided a protective hedge around them enabling the country to prosper beyond their grandest dreams.

"I am sure that never was a people who had more reason to acknowledge a Divine interposition in their affairs, than those of the United States, and I should be pained to believe that they have forgotten that agency, which so often manifested during the Revolution or that they failed to consider the omnipotence of that God who is alone able to protect them."

-George Washington - March 11, 1792

Chapter Five

America Was A Nation Protected By God's Hedge

John Cotton died in 1652. He was a Puritan scholar and clergyman who greatly influenced the destiny of Puritan New England. Principles stated in his sermons were frequently put into immediate practice by civil authorities. John Cotton declared:

> What He hath planted, He will maintain. Every plantation His right hand hath not planted shall be rooted up, but His own plantation shall prosper and flourish.
>
> When He promiseth peace and safety, what enemies shall be able to make the promise of God of none effect? Neglect not wall and bulwarks and fortifications for your own defense, but ever let the name of the Lord be your strong tower, and the word of His promise, the rock of your refuge.
>
> His word that made heaven and earth will not fail, till heaven and earth be no more...If God make a covenant to be a God to thee and thine, then it is thy part to see to it that thy children and servants be God's people.[31]

Scripture teaches that God provided hedges of protection around people and nations that seek to honor Him. In Job 1 and 2 the hedge of

57

protection that surrounded Job is described. In a unique picture of an encounter between God and the "accuser of the brethren," Satan, God poses the intriguing question, "Have you considered my servant Job?" (Job 1:8). He goes on to commend Job:

> "I have no one on earth like him, he is blameless and upright, a man who fears God and shuns evil." To which Satan responds, "Does Job fear God for nothing? Have you not put a hedge around him and his household and everything he has so that his flocks and herds are spread throughout the land. But stretch out your hand and strike everything he has and he will curse you to your face" (Job 1:9-10).

There are a number of important truths revealed in this important exchange between the two opposing forces that stand behind every occurrence that takes place on this earth.

God's Awesome Power protects Job

First, notice the awesome power of our great God and the contrasting impotence of our enemy Satan. I learned during my formal theological training at Southwestern Baptist Theological Seminary in Ft. Worth that there are three distinguishing attributes that God alone possesses. He is omnipotent, omnipresent and omniscient. Simply stated, God is all-powerful, all-present, and all-knowing, and He is all three, all of the time.

Now, contrast that with Satan. He is limited in power, is limited to one place at any given moment, and has limited knowledge. Job 1 reveals that Satan can only operate within the framework of God's permission. Listen carefully to Satan's response to God concerning Job: "Have you not put a hedge around him and his household and everything he has?" In other words, Satan is saying, "Of course, I have considered him, but I can't touch him. You won't let me."

Second, notice the extent of this hedge around Job.
- it was around his *person*, "Have you not put a hedge around him."
- it was around his *people*, "...and his household."
- it was around his *possessions*, "...and everything he has?"
- it was around his *profession*, "You have blessed the work of his hands..."

The protection of God extended over Job's person, his people, his possessions and his profession. Satan, who makes it his business to corrupt and destroy people, made the unmistakable admission that he could not touch Job, because Job found favor in God's sight. The remaining chapters of Job reveal why God so delighted in and favored Job. It was because Job was a man of commitment and character. In fact, if you study Job 1 and 2 carefully, God allows you to catch a glimpse of the depth of Job's walk with God. Satan wrongfully assumed that Job loved God because of all that God had done for him, but God knew Job's love went far deeper than that. God knew that Job loved God because of who He was, not because of what He had done.

Job Was A Man Of Consecration

In chapter one, in our first encounter with Job, we find him rising early in the morning to intercede for his children. Rather than assuming the role of the naive father who thinks his kids are perfect, Job rose early and prayed for his children, assuming their potential for failure was in fact always present. "Perhaps my children have sinned and cursed God in their hearts" (Job 1:5). Was this a passing fancy? The Scripture doesn't leave us wondering. It goes on to state, "This was Job's regular custom."

Dads, is it your regular custom to rise up early and intercede for your children? God knew He had a winner in Job. He knew Job was a man he could depend on. So much so, he allowed Satan to level an all-out assault on Job. The remaining portion of the first chapter of Job documents Satan's furious attack on Job's household.

There are enormous lessons to be learned here. It is clear who is in charge. As we move through this world system it is easy to be seduced into believing that Satan must be in charge; especially when you consider the extent to which the devastation of sin and its consequences have pervaded our nation. Job 1 reminds us that Satan only operates within the specific guidelines put forth by our great God.

First, he was granted permission to touch Job's oxen and donkeys, and did he ever. Satan engineered an attack of the Sabeans to kill Job's servants and steal his oxen and donkeys (v. 14).

Second, God granted Satan permission to touch Job's sheep. Satan caused lightning to fall from the sky and burn up the sheep and their attending shepherds (v. 16).

Third, God gave Satan permission to touch Job's herds of camels.

Satan incited the Chaldeans to swoop down on the herdsmen and kill them and steal his camels (v. 17).

Finally, God gave Satan permission to touch Job's ten children. Satan manipulated a mighty storm in the desert that toppled the structure where Job's children were celebrating in their older brother's house, and the house collapsed, killing them all (vs. 18-19).

In one brief, terrifying day, Satan destroyed what had taken Job a lifetime to build. Suddenly, without warning, Job, the greatest of all the peoples of the East, was financially devastated and facing a bleak future without his seven sons and three daughters.

Satan Is The Architect Of Destruction

Satan did to Job what Satan, unrestrained by our gracious and loving God, would do to every human being on the face of the earth. John 10:10 reveals Satan's strategy for all; "...the thief (Satan) comes only to steal and kill and destroy." There is a day coming when he will have free reign on the earth to carry out his designs. In fact, the only thing that restrains him now is God, by the power and presence of His Holy Spirit. Paul speaks of a day, perhaps soon to come, when the restraint will be removed. "For the secret power of lawlessness is already at work, but the one who now holds it back will continue to do so till he is taken out of the way" (II Thessalonians 2:7).

I believe that the presence of the Holy Spirit, who will suddenly disappear at the time of the rapture of the Church, is what is spoken of here. But let me hasten to make a point which will become increasingly clear as we make our way through this book. The reason there has been so much pervasive evil so openly portrayed in America during the past thirty years, is largely due to the silence of the Church. Edmund Burke is credited with stating: "All that is necessary for evil to triumph is for good men to do nothing." Jesus said:

> "You are the salt of the earth. But if the salt loses its saltiness, how can it be made salty again. It is no longer good for anything, except to be thrown out and trampled by men. You are the light of the world. A city on a hill cannot be hidden. Neither do people light a lamp and put it under a bowl. Instead they put it on its stand, and it gives light to everyone in the house. In the same way, let your light shine before men, that they may see your good deeds and praise your Father in heaven" (Matthew 5:13-16).

The Church has ceased being salt and light in America. No longer are we a restraining force against sin. We have been guilty of allowing the world system to set the agenda. Christians have in large measure retreated to their church buildings where we have preached to ourselves, while the framers of public debate often ignore us altogether. America has become schizophrenic. While the majority of Americans hold deeply to their faith in God, a comparatively small group of humanists have been allowed to secularize our nation.

Make no mistake about it, Satan hates God and Satan hates you. The only reason he has not assaulted you and your family more than he has is because of God's restraining hand. That is why it is imperative that we walk as Job walked. How did Job respond to such assault?

> "At this, Job got up and tore his robe and shaved his head. Then he fell to the ground in worship and said: 'Naked I came from my mother's womb and naked I will depart. The LORD gave and the LORD has taken away; May the name of the LORD be praised.' In all this, Job did not sin by charging God with wrongdoing" (Job 1:20-22).

I have three great children. When I consider what happened to Job's family and relate that to my own, the depth of Job's commitment to trust in the sovereignty of God overwhelms me. Did the Lord receive glory from Job's response? You be the judge. Job was written thousands of years ago, but his testimony continues to glorify God until the present hour. I make no pretense that I have arrived at that level of commitment. I cannot say my faith is strong enough to respond in such complete abandonment to God. God alone knows how I would respond, but I do know this; it will require that level of commitment to recapture this nation for Christ.

Job Was A Man Of Integrity

But wait, Satan was not through. Neither was God. Job 2 reveals that again Satan, the accuser of the brethren, was in the presence of God. And again, it is as if God is saying, "Satan, I have heard your endless accusations against my children, but what about Job? Have you considered my servant Job?"

In fact, if you read the text in chapter two, it looks like a reprint of chapter one, with one small but significant difference. Again, the Lord describes Job in the following manner, "There is no one on earth like him; he is blameless and upright, a man who fears God and shuns evil." But next comes the most important line in the text. Of Job, God says, "And still he maintains his integrity, though you incited me to ruin him without any reason" (Job 2:3).

We often hear public speakers introduced with all manner of accolades and glowing remarks. I have been to a few funerals where I wanted to walk over to the casket while the preacher was preaching, and look in to make sure he was talking about the same man I knew. It is amazing how much everyone improves after they are dead.

God does not exaggerate, Job really was blameless. That does not mean he was sinless. It means that every sin had been confessed and repented of and atoned for. Job really was upright. We Texans might say, he was a straight shooter, he was the same every day, in every life situation. Job was the real McCoy. Job feared God, which is why he shunned evil. Job lived with the continual understanding that he would someday stand before a holy, righteous God and give an account of his life.

God knew that, but He wanted Satan and all of antiquity to also know it. Job was a man of **integrity**. *Webster's Unabridged Dictionary* defines integrity in the following manner: "moral soundness or purity; incorruptness; uprightness; honesty."

God builds hedges around men of integrity. Today, there are far too many men with reputation (what men say about you) and far too few men with integrity (what God knows about you).

Gentlemen, integrity is what God is looking for. Men who have considered the claims of Christ, looked fully at the allurement of the world, counted the cost, and decided to go with God.

Satan continues to miss the point with Job. He is convinced that Job has a price. "Skin for skin!" Satan replied, "A man will give all he has for his own life. But stretch out your hand and strike his flesh and bones, and he will surely curse you to your face" (Job 2:4-5).

Because God knew Job's heart was true, he responded by saying, "Very well then, he is in your hands" (Job 2:6). Now Satan is given the opportunity to even strike the **person** of Job. It appears the hedge is completely removed. But a closer look reveals the hedge is still there, "...but you must spare his life" (Job 2:6b).

Satan has much power in today's world, but it is always limited by the Lord God of Heaven. Manley Beasley, a wonderful evangelist and friend, went to be with the Lord in 1990. He greatly impacted my life with his ministry. He used to often say of Satan that he is nothing more than the messenger boy of God. I believe that statement accurately reflects the power of Satan in comparison to our great God. As long as we live in proper relationship to our Savior, Satan has no authority over our lives beyond that which God allows.

Look at the venomous hate Satan pours upon Job once he is granted access. "So Satan went out from the presence of the Lord and afflicted Job with painful sores from the soles of his feet to the top of his head" (Job 2:7). As Job sat in his misery, doing his best to doctor his infected body, his wife said to him, "Are you still holding on to your integrity? Curse God and die!" (Job 2:9).

It has been said, when you squeeze a man, what's inside comes out. When Job was squeezed, we discover that he was a man of integrity. He replied, "...You are talking like a foolish woman. Shall we accept good from God, and not trouble? In all this Job did not sin in what he said." Jesus said, "For out of the overflow of the heart, the mouth speaks." Clearly, in the overflow of Job's heart was a desire to glorify God. Equally clear is Satan's desire to destroy Job.

The Hedge Around The Nation

Not only does God build hedges around individuals and their families, but He also builds hedges around nations that fear and acknowledge Him. Deuteronomy 28 records a covenant that God made with Israel. In this chapter He guarantees the nation success as long as they acknowledge Him. "If you fully obey the Lord your God and carefully follow his commands...." Furthermore He promised in Deuteronomy 28:1-2 to set them "high above all the nations on the earth" if they would simply obey the Lord. God also made a second guarantee; He guaranteed their destruction. "If you do not obey the Lord your God and do not carefully follow all his commands and decrees I am giving you today, all these curses will come upon you and overtake you" (Deuteronomy 28:15).

God made a number of specific promises to Israel that were conditional upon their obeying and acknowledging Him. The founders of America believed that those promises would be equally applied to them if they sought to glorify God in the building of their new nation. Study the list of promised blessings in Deuteronomy 28 and judge for yourself whether or not they seem to apply to America:

1) You will be blessed in the city and you will be blessed in the country (v. 3)

(Example: Prosperity throughout the nation).

2) The fruit of your womb will be blessed (v. 4)
   (Example: Healthy and godly children).

3) The crops of your land will be blessed (v. 4)
   (Example: America is the breadbasket of the world.).

4) Your calves and your lambs will be blessed (v. 4)
   (Example: Fertile grazing lands, producing healthy and bountiful herds).

5) Your basket and your kneading trough will be blessed (v. 5)
   (Example: Strong and prosperous industry).

6) You will be blessed when you go in and when you go out (v. 6)
   (Example: Freedom of travel).

7) Your enemies will be defeated (v. 7)
   (Example: America never lost a war until Vietnam.).

8) The Lord will send a blessing on your barn and everything you do (v. 8)
   (Example: Abundant prosperity).

9) The Lord will bless you in the land He is giving you (v. 8)
   (Example: Health and wealth).

10) The Lord will establish you as a holy people (v. 9)
    (Example: Read the testimony of Alexis de Tocqueville, pg. 65).

11) Then all the peoples on the earth will see that you are called by the name of the Lord and they will fear you (v. 10)
    (Example: America's prominence throughout the world).

12) The Lord will grant you abundant prosperity (v. 11)
    (Example: America has the highest living standard in the world).

13) The Lord will open the heavens, the storehouse of His bounty, to send rain on your land in season and to bless all the work of your hands (v. 12)
    (Example: Favorable climates produces bountiful harvests).

14) You will lend to many nations but will borrow from none (v. 12)
    (Example: America never accumulated debt until the early '60s).

15) The Lord will make you the head and not the tail...You will always be at the top, never at the bottom (v. 13)
    (Example: America is the leader of the free world.).

It is clear to me that just as God blessed Israel and used her as a city set upon a hill to reflect His power, glory, and dominion to all the earth in an ancient generation, He again exalted another nation, the United States of America, to show the world how He rewards those who wholeheartedly devote themselves to Him. When you consider what finally evolved from the faith of that small band of Pilgrims who came to America on the Mayflower, how could anyone be so arrogant as to deny that God did not will it to happen. Our ancestors knew that America was a precious gift from God and unashamedly said so. We must again recognize who we are, and take America back out of the hands of those who deny His laws and precepts and choose to ignore history.

America has not been lucky, she has been blessed. She is the product of the determination of our forebearers to forge a nation built upon biblical principles. As they labored to create a Christian nation, God looked with affection and favor upon their efforts and gave them supernatural guidance that enabled them to author foundational documents unlike any the world had ever seen before. The wisdom of our Declaration of Independence and Constitution can only be described as inspired. Truly, the hand of God was driving the thoughts and decisions of those men.

Why God Removes The Hedge

During the French Revolution of the 1790's, influential scholars and infidels attempted to prove that morality could be maintained without religion. Soon, the streets of France were like rivers of blood. In the 1960's, liberal college professors began conveying this same wicked lie to college students across America. In 1962, The Supreme Court followed suit, ruling in the *Engel v. Vitale* case that children could no longer pray in public schools. This ruling ushered in an unprecedented era of antireligious activism in our courts. As we shall see, the results of this frontal assault on religion has resulted in America becoming a nation without a soul.

Alexis de Tocqueville was a famous French Statesman, historian and social philosopher. Beginning in 1831, he and a friend toured the countrysides of America for the purpose of observing the American people and their institutions. In 1835 and 1840, he published a two part work entitled *Democracy in America*. His observations are invaluable. The following are but a few of his remarks, but they are full of insight:

> Upon my arrival in the United States the religious aspect of the country was the first thing that struck my attention; and the longer I stayed there, the more I perceived the great political consequences resulting from this new state of things.
>
> In France, I had almost always seen the spirit of religion and

the spirit of freedom marching in opposite directions. But in America I found they were intimately united and that they reigned in common over the same country."

Religion in America...must be regarded as the foremost of the political institutions of that country; for if it does not impart a taste for freedom, it facilitates the use of it. Indeed, it is in this same point of view that the inhabitants of the United States themselves look upon religious belief.

I do not know whether all Americans have a sincere faith in their religion - for who can search the human heart? - But I am certain that they hold it to be indispensable to the maintenance of republican institutions. This opinion is not peculiar to a class of citizens or a party, but it belongs to the whole nation and to every rank of society.

The sects that exist in the United States are innumerable. They all differ in respect to the worship which is due to the Creator; but they all agree in respect to the duties which are due from man to man.

Each sect adores the Deity in its own peculiar manner, but all sects preach the same moral law in the name of God...Moreover, all the sects of the United States are comprised within the great unity of Christianity, and Christian morality is everywhere the same."

In the United States the sovereign authority is religious,...there is no country in the world where the Christian religion retains a greater influence over the souls of men than in America, and there can be no greater proof of its utility and of its conformity to human nature than that its influence is powerfully felt over the most enlightened and free nation of the earth.

In the United States, if a political character attacks a sect [denomination], this may not prevent even the partisans of that very sect, from supporting him; but if he attacks all the sects together [Christianity], every one abandons him and he remains alone.

I do not question that the great austerity of manners that is observable in the United States arises, in the first instance, from religious faith...its influence over the mind of woman is supreme, and women are the protectors of morals. There is certainly no country in the world where the tie of marriage is more respected than in America or where conjugal happiness is more highly or worthily appreciated...

In the United States the influence of religion is not confined to the manners, but it extends to the intelligence of the people...Christianity, therefore reigns without obstacle, by universal consent; the consequence is, as I have before observed, that every principle of the moral world is fixed and determinate...

I sought for the key to the greatness and genius of America in her harbors...; in her fertile fields and boundless forests; in her rich mines and vast world commerce; in her public school system and institutions of learning. I sought for it in her democratic Congress and in her matchless Constitution.

Not until I went into the churches of America and heard her pulpits flame with righteousness did I understand the secret of her genius and power. America is great because America is good, and if America ever ceases to be good, America will cease to be great.

The safeguard of morality is religion, and morality is the best security of law as well as the surest pledge of freedom.

The Americans combine the notions of Christianity and of liberty so intimately in their minds, that it is impossible to make them conceive the one without the other.

Christianity is the companion of liberty in all its conflicts - the cradle of its infancy, and the divine source of its claims.

They brought with them...a form of Christianity, which I cannot better describe, than by styling it a democratic and republican religion...From the earliest settlement of the emigrants, politics and religion contracted an alliance which has never been dissolved.[32]

What would Alexis de Tocqueville write were he to visit America today? In the fifth chapter of Isaiah, the prophet relates the song of the vineyard:

"I will sing for the one I love a song about his vineyard: My loved one had a vineyard on a fertile hillside. He dug it up and cleared it of stones and planted it with the choicest vines. He built a watchtower in it and cut out a winepress as well. Then he looked for a crop of good grapes, but it yielded only bad fruit. Now you dwellers in Jerusalem and men of Judah, judge between me and my vineyard. What more could have been done for my vineyard than I have done for it? When I looked for good grapes, why did it yield only bad? Now I will tell you what I am going to do to my vineyard: I will take away its hedge, and it will be destroyed; I will break down its wall, and it will be trampled. I will make it a wasteland, neither pruned nor cultivated, and briers and thorns will grow there. I will command the clouds not to rain on it. The vineyard of the Lord Almighty is the house of Israel, and the men of Judah are the garden of his delight. And he looked for justice, but saw bloodshed; for righteousness, but heard cries of distress" (Isaiah 5:1-7).

In verse five, the prophet relates an awesome word of judgment: "I will take away its hedge and it will be destroyed." Isaiah understood that no nation can survive once God's protective hedge is removed.

Three Reasons For Removing The Hedge

There are at least three reasons why God lowers or removes the hedge from around individuals and nations.

First, the hedge is lowered for **discipline.** There are times in the life of a nation, as there are times in the life of men, when God incrementally lowers the hedge to allow Satan to invoke misery and suffering, as a direct result of sin. The author of Hebrews writes: "My son, do not make light of the Lord's discipline, and do not lose heart when he rebukes you, because the Lord disciplines those he loves, and he punishes everyone he accepts as a son. Endure hardship as discipline; God is treating you as sons. For what son is not disciplined by his father? If you are not disciplined (and everyone undergoes discipline) then you are illegitimate children and not true sons" (Hebrews 12:5-8).

God's intent during such times is that we return in humble repentance to Him. I learned, as a child, that the best thing to do when my father whipped me with his belt, was to run to him rather than away from him. I discovered that when I clung to his legs, he had to hit himself too, and he would soon stop, stoop down, and gather me in his arms. Our Heavenly Father responds in the same way when a person or a nation returns to Him.

I am convinced that the Civil War was a time in the life of our nation when God lowered the hedge. God could not ignore the national sin of slavery. The Civil War resulted in the death of hundreds of thousands of

American men, women and children. The hedge was lowered, and Satan came in "to steal, kill and destroy" (John 10:10).

Second, the hedge is lowered for **discipleship.** By that, I mean for the purpose of revealing to others the depth of the love of God or the character of the one undergoing trial. I believe this was the case in Job's trial. God was unveiling the depth of Job's character for all to see. There are incredible lessons about suffering, endurance, perseverance and patience taught in the book of Job.

In John 9, the disciples asked Jesus whether it was the man's own sin or that of his parents that caused the man to be born blind. Jesus replied, "Neither this man nor his parents sinned, but this happened so that the work of God might be displayed in his life." Jesus was about to disciple His followers, both then and throughout the ages to follow, through the lessons He was about to teach. The hedge had been lowered in an innocent man's life allowing Satan to inflict blindness so that God could reveal the Messiah to a lost and hopeless world. Be cautious about assuming when someone is suffering that it is the result of some unconfessed and perhaps secret sin.

Third, the hedge is lowered for **destruction.** "A man who remains stiff-necked after many rebukes will suddenly be destroyed without remedy" (Proverbs 29:1). If a man refuses to heed God's discipline, God will lower the hedge further until the man is destroyed. The same principle applies to nations. It is my belief that America stands on the brink of such destruction if God's people do not respond swiftly, completely and humbly. It is now close to midnight for our country.

A Personal Testimony

I graduated from high school in 1968. The sitcom, "Happy Days," could have been filmed on our high school campus. Richey, Potsey, Ralph and Fonzi all went to Galena Park High School. Well, not literally, but each fictitious character could have been depicting someone I knew.

It is hard for me to imagine how anyone could have enjoyed growing up more than I. In high school, I was involved in everything from athletics to student government, where I was president of our student body. Across America, there was growing social unrest, and I was fully aware of Vietnam (my draft number was 247, as I recall), but somehow, none of that affected me.

In 1966, our high school integrated without incident. The only black high school in our school district was Fidelity Manor, a perennial playoff contender in football, and we simply absorbed them into our high school. One of their star athletes, who became a high school all-American in 1968, made integration appealing in Galena Park because he was such a great athlete and person. There was racial unrest in the lower grades, but in high school, the transition was without incident.

As president of our student body in 1968, it was my duty to meet in the principal's office each morning at 8:25 a.m., along with the president of the Christian Student's Union. Every morning the two of us led the student body, over the public address system, in the pledge of allegiance to the flag, a Bible reading, and prayer for the day. No one ever wondered if we should do that. It was simply understood, that's how the day began.

In the fall of that year, I went to Stephen F. Austin University in Nacogdoches, Texas, on a full scholarship to play football. Never one to lack purpose in life, I immediately declared a major in Political Science and began pursuing my goal of obtaining a law degree to facilitate my life ambition to enter politics. (I received a higher calling along the way.)

I got very active in student government and was elected Vice President of the freshman class. It has often been said that East Texans are a little behind the times. The radicalism that was inundating college campuses across America throughout the '60s was just beginning to surface at S.F.A. in 1968.

The Political Science Department was very liberal. For the first time in my life, I began hearing professors attack everything I held sacred and dear. Suddenly, nothing seemed secure. Day after day, my entire belief system and everything I believed America stood for was held in contempt, or at least, suspect. My core values were constantly being assaulted, and by the very adults I had been taught by my parents to revere and respect.

During the summer between my freshman and sophomore years, I made a radical recommitment of my life to the Lordship of Jesus Christ. This commitment provided an anchor for my beliefs that I desperately needed. For the first time in my life, I became an activist Christian. Suddenly, I developed a passion for sharing my faith, and when I returned to school that fall, I got very active in several Christian organizations on campus. The S.F.A. Chapter of the Fellowship of Christian Athletes elected me to be their president.

Word soon spread across campus that there was an athlete "on fire for Jesus." Our squad was quite successful that season, leading the nation in total offense and attaining national ranking. This opened a number of doors for me to speak and share my faith as the starting center for the Lumberjacks. (I love to remind people where I speak that I made the former, all-pro, place-kicker for the world champion Washington Redskins, Mark Mosley, famous. How? In college, I hiked almost every ball he kicked, en route to becoming an N.F.L. star.)

Soon, the word even reached my very liberal Political Science professors that they had a "rednecked conservative," Christian athlete in their class. I began to discover a little of what the early Christians must have felt when they found themselves in the arenas of Rome, facing hungry lions. Ph.D.'s began trying to make sport of the "Christian."

I shall never forget the day that I sat in Dr. Steele's 8:00 a.m. class, when just after he called the roll of about forty students, he again called out my name; "Mr. Scarborough," the words rang out as my heart skipped a beat. "I hear you are a Christian!"

"Yes Sir," I replied, wondering where this was leading, but really quite proud that my name was being so associated with the name of Christ.

He then asked, as he leaned on his lectern, peering over the top of his reading glasses, "Do you know what Karl Marx said about religion?"

Frankly, as a sophomore in college, I was not even sure who Karl Marx was, so I replied, "No."

He then proceeded to tell us that Karl Marx, one of the fathers of Communism, believed that religion was the "opiate of the masses." He then asked, "What do you say to that?"

In perhaps my defining moment in college, God supernaturally revealed to me the perfect answer. (I am not that smart!) I replied, to his disbelief, "I agree with him."

In confusion, he responded, "How can you agree with him? You are a Christian!"

I then proceeded to give a verbal witness to Dr. Steele and forty open-eared students, "I do not have religion, Dr. Steele, I have discovered a relationship with Jesus Christ that has changed my life."

Dr. Steele dropped the discussion and continued on with his lecture. Without question, he had not anticipated such an answer. After class, I stopped by his office and requested an appointment. Later, over coffee, I discovered that Dr. Steele had at one time pursued a theological degree, fully intending to go into the ministry, but a liberal professor had shattered his faith and he instead, opted to teach. I am convinced I struck a chord in his heart that day. Only God knows for sure.

Bill and Hillary Bought In

I made it though college unaffected by the liberal, anti-American gobbledygook I heard every day, and lived the next ten to fifteen years believing that surely no one really embraced such amoral teachings. Later, in the eighties, I began to realize that many apparently did. Abraham Lincoln said, "the lectures in our colleges in one generation become the laws of the next."

The sixties were a uniquely radical time, unlike anything that had preceded them. Bill and Hillary Clinton are products of that era. Unfortunately, they bought into the liberal philosophies that were being espoused, completely. When I turned eighteen, I dutifully registered for the draft, went to Baytown, Texas, took my physical, received my lottery number, and decided if my number came up, I would not like it, but I would go to Vietnam and serve my country.

We now know that Bill Clinton decided, "if my number comes up, I'll do everything within my power to escape service." During his college tenure he conducted protests against his government while in Europe and visited Moscow. During the first six months of his Presidency, he identified himself as a liberal social activist, signing Presidential Orders facilitating the slaughter of innocent unborn children at our military complexes around the world, and legitimizing homosexual behavior. He became the first president in history to place known homosexuals in key positions of policy making throughout his administration.

What More Can God Do?

Deuteronomy 28 describes the blessings that follow national obedience to God's law. As we shall see in the second section of this book, the hedge of protection around America has been lowered, and when the hedge is lowered, Satan is free to administer destruction. God is our greatest hope. He is also our greatest threat. Our response in the immediate future will determine which He will be to America. We will experience a national revival or we will see the end of the American experiment with freedom. Let us not forget His promise:

> "If my people, who are called by my name, will humble them-selves and pray and seek my face and turn from their wicked ways, then will I hear from heaven and will forgive their sin and will heal their land" (II Chronicles 7:14).

In Isaiah 5, God asks a probing question of the nation of Judah that

I believe could just as appropriately be asked of America today: "What more could have been done for my vineyard than I have done for it? When I looked for good grapes why did it yield only bad?" (Isaiah 5:4).

I cannot help but think that God must be asking that same question of you and me this very moment. Many of our founding fathers believed the conditional promises of Deuteronomy 28 applied to them as much as to Israel. They also believed the conditional curses would apply to them if they departed from their commitment to honor God.

In the next section, I intend to validate my conviction that America is under the judgment hand of God. I believe many, if not all, of the curses of Deuteronomy 28 are now surfacing in our nation. You can evaluate for yourself as to how completely these curses pervade our beloved country. Do I believe we are beyond hope? If I did, I would not be writing this book. As I stated at the outset, aspects of this book may be very discouraging, but in the end, it is about hope. Our God is a God abounding in mercy. He is the God of the second chance. May we, like Nineveh of old, repent.

Read carefully the words of Deuteronomy 28:15: "However, if you do not obey the LORD your God and do not carefully follow all his commands and decrees I am giving you today, all these curses will come upon you and overtake you..."

1) Your basket and kneading trough will be cursed (v. 17) (Example: failing industry).

2) The fruit of your womb will be cursed (v. 18) (Example: the loss of fertility due to venereal diseases and abortion. This could also allude to youth violence.).

3) The crops of your lands will be cursed (v. 18; 38-40) (Example: fires, droughts and floods in America's heart-land.).

4) Your calves and lambs will be cursed (v. 18) (Example: falling prices and rising costs.).

5) Confusion surrounding everything you do (v. 20) (Example: mental disorders).

6) The Lord will plague you with...the Lord will strike you with wasting disease. (v. 21-22) (Example: venereal disease, AIDS, new viral infections, etc.).

7) Scorching heat and drought (v. 22) (Example: declining water tables).

8) The Lord will turn the rain into dust...it will (then) come

down, until you are destroyed (v. 24)
(Example: hurricanes, tornadoes, floods and violent weather patterns, etc.).

9) The Lord will cause you to be defeated on the battlefields (v. 25)
(Example: Vietnam).

10) The Lord will afflict you with tumors and festering sores (v. 27)
(Example: cancer and AIDS).

11) The Lord will afflict you with madness...confusion of mind (v.28)
(Example: mental disorder).

12) You will be oppressed and robbed (v. 29)
(Example: the crime explosion).

13) You will be pledged to be married...but another will take her (v. 30)
(Example: the breakdown of marriage and growing infidelity).

14) The alien who lives among you will rise above you higher and higher (v. 43)
(Example: immigration difficulties).

15) He will lend to you but you will not lend to him (v. 44)
(Example: the growing national debt).

Moses concluded these warnings with a solemn and distressingly applicable statement: "All these curses will come upon you because you did not obey the Lord...Because you did not serve the Lord joyfully and gladly in the time of prosperity" (Deuteronomy 28:45;47).

In the next section, we will study in depth the judgment that befell Jerusalem and Judah as a result of the nation's failure to depend on God. Nine chapters will be devoted to nine specific sins that befall any nation that forgets God. Isaiah the prophet, in chapter three of his prophecy, announced to Jerusalem and Judah that He would remove their supply and support... "See now, the Lord, the Lord Almighty is about to take from Jerusalem and Judah both supply and support."

The chapter then lists nine specific supports that will be taken away. I believe all nine supports have been removed or diminished in America. God is calling committed men to repair the wall and restore America to her Christian heritage.

"No power over the freedom of religion... (is) delegated to the United States by the Constitution."

-Thomas Jefferson, 1798

Chapter Six

Conquered By The Courts

In our generation, we have been privileged to see firsthand the moral vacuum that atheistic communism produced in Russia as the Iron Curtain was removed, revealing a nation without a soul. Yet, while millions are coming to Christ in former communist bloc countries, and religious leaders like Bill Gothard are being enlisted to teach biblical values in the public school system of the former Soviet Union, we in America continue to hear of case after case where American citizens are forbidden to express their faith. At a graduation ceremony in Salt Lake City, Utah, this past May (1995), the Tenth Circuit Court of Appeals issued a restraining order against West High School students, forbidding the Acapella Choir from singing two traditional songs, because they contained the words "Lord" and "God."

The parents of sixteen-year-old Rachel Bachman claimed in their lawsuit that the names "Lord" and "God" referred to the Christian God and therefore, the song constituted a prayer which violated the First Amendment. The Court agreed. One has to wonder how long it will be before a liberal Federal Judge declares the phrase, "One Nation Under God," contained in our "Pledge of Allegiance," is constitutionally unacceptable.

Cal Thomas, in his syndicated column, reports that one of the students, William Badger, led in a small populist rebellion as he got on stage at the graduation ceremony and invited the audience to join him in singing one of the banned songs, "Friends," that included the scandalous lyrics "Friends are friends forever if the Lord's the Lord of them." In a day when drug abuse is at epidemic levels, and gangs are beginning to control our public schools, it is hard to imagine adults being offended by high school seniors singing such songs. I wonder if the lyrics of a Madonna song, or Snoopy Doggy Dog would have been deemed offensive?

The high school Principal, Bill Boston, attempted to silence the crowd. Badger was physically removed from the stage and not allowed to participate in the graduation exercise. (I'd be interested in knowing what offenses other seniors were forgiven of who did participate.) Thomas goes on to report the administration officials were planning to study video tapes of the ceremony to identify underclassmen who participated and perhaps punish them and assign them community service projects for their offensive behavior. This sounds more like the old Soviet Union than America.

What no one seems to understand or remember is that God is an observer to all these events and thousands more that never receive national attention. In America, about the only thing censored today is Christianity, the same Christianity that was the driving force behind the building of this great nation. We are all the recipients of God's blessings upon our forebearers.

The Constitutional Revolution of F.D.R.

It is generally agreed that our judicial branch of government entered a new era under Franklin D. Roosevelt. Though I make no pretense to be a legal scholar, the observations I am about to offer have been reported by many who are.

During Roosevelt's Presidency, a number of key elements in what Roosevelt termed his "New Deal," were struck down by the Supreme Court as being beyond the reach of the federal government. Roosevelt and his chief advisors, including Attorney General Homer Cummings, were stunned. "We have been relegated to the horse and buggy definition of interstate commerce," Roosevelt proclaimed. Cummings responded by saying, "I tell you, Mr. President, they mean to destroy us...We will have to find a way to get rid of the present membership of the Supreme Court."[33]

In a series of adverse decisions, the Supreme Court invalidated the heart of President Roosevelt's "New Deal" plans for national economic recovery. In a unanimous ruling, they declared Roosevelt's "National Industrial Recovery Act" unconstitutional. A later ruling invalidated the "Agricultural Adjustment Act," on the grounds it encroached on regulatory powers reserved to the states by the Tenth Amendment.

This launched what has been dubbed "The Constitutional Revolution in the Age of Roosevelt." Roosevelt began to systematically "reform" the court. His critics called it "court packing." Time and circumstances favored Roosevelt. By the time he died in 1945, he had named eight of the nine sitting Supreme Court Justices, filling vacancies caused by death or retirement.

Roosevelt's judicial activism cleared the path for his legislative agenda. From 1937 forward, not one piece of significant national or state socioeconomic legislation was struck down. Roosevelt's strategy served his legislative agenda well, but unfortunately he also politicized the High Court.

The Living Constitution

Since that revolution, the Court has evolved. For the past forty years, a number of justices have been appointed who view their role less as an interpreter of the Constitution and more as a manipulator of the Constitution. As possessors of a worldview that denies the existence of a Supreme Being, many hold a subconscious disdain for the "unenlightened" who still cling to their antiquated and discredited faith. They reject that biblical revelation reveals certain "absolutes" from which mankind cannot deviate. They find it outside reason to interpret the Constitution as a fixed document, and therefore must manipulate it to fit their philosophical positions.

Because these men and women are well-educated and have been trained to think logically, an explanation for such a radical departure from the forebearers is essential. The rational tool to provide them with an honorable escape is to certify the Constitution as a "living" document. "Living," means "changing." Hence, the document can be manipulated to fit within the philosophical framework of the justices. In 1962, with growing rapidity, the Supreme Court issued ruling after ruling that reversed the meaning of the First Amendment and made a mockery of the intent of its writers.

Today's legal scholars are continually debating how to interpret and apply the Constitution in today's world. In scholastic circles, two main schools of thought drive the discussion, with dozens of subcategories within each school. "Interpretivism" embodies the notion that judges should confine themselves to enforcing norms that are either stated or clearly implied in the written Constitution. "Noninterpretivism" reflects the view that the courts should go beyond the stated and clearly implicit norms of the Constitution and, when necessary, disregard the specific intent of the framers in order to promote justice. The inherent danger in adopting the "noninterpretivism" approach is that it gives unlimited power to nonelected judges. This approach to administering the Constitution appeals to judges because it empowers them to inject their personal views into society, backed by the supposed authority of the U.S. Constitution. This view has dominated the judicial elite of our nation for the past generation. The result is that America is now like Israel in the days of the Judges, when: "In those days Israel had no king; everyone did as he saw fit" (Judges 21:25).

Legal scholars defend "noninterpretivism" on the grounds that strict "interpretivism" would not have resulted in the court's decisions to end racial segregation and discrimination against women. That argument is suspect in light of the fact that our founding fathers designed other means for correcting such societal sins through the legislative process. While "noninterpretivism" has addressed these wrongs more expediently than the legislative process could have, it has also resulted in such abominable decisions as to allow unborn American citizens to be slaughtered through the ninth month of pregnancy, and their bodies to be dismembered and experimented on as if they were laboratory rodents, under the auspices of "fetal tissue research." Soon this relativistic approach, if not arrested, will discover a "constitutional right" to exterminate the unwanted old and terminally ill. What must a Holy God be thinking?

The Big Lie

In July of 1995, President Clinton suddenly made the bold pronouncement that the framers of our Constitution never intended to prevent our children from participating in noncoerced private prayers while at school. This sudden warmth to the Religious Right's deeply held belief that prayer must again be allowed and welcomed in our public schools has sent mixed signals throughout the Christian community. I believe Mr. Clinton's remarks were more inspired by politics than a reflection of a deeply held moral commitment to again exalt our Great God in America. This belief was bolstered when the American Civil Liberties Union endorsed his comments. As a general practice, if they are for something, I am against it. I have discovered that typically, my Christian convictions will lead me to the opposite position of that held by the ACLU.

Immediately following Clinton's assertion, a public school teacher asked me, "Pastor, does this mean I can pray in my classroom?" That question illustrates the confusion that has pervaded our nation since the Supreme Court ruled that a simple, innocent twenty-two word prayer, that had been offered daily for many years in a New York school, was unconstitutional in the now famous *Engel v. Vitale* case of 1962. The controversial prayer simply stated:

Almighty God, we acknowledge our dependence upon Thee, and we beg Thy blessings upon us, our parents, our teachers and our Country.[34]

By ruling that the prayer was unconstitutional, the High Court was saying it was against the will and design of the framers of the Constitution. Amazingly, no one was compelled to participate in the prayer. It was simply a tradition of the school. Clearly it was a "nondenominational" prayer. However, the Supreme Court ruling stated:

Neither the fact that the prayer may be denominationally neutral nor the fact that its observance on the part of the students is voluntary, can serve to free it from the limitations of the First (Amendment)...Prayer in the public school system breaches the constitutional wall of separation between the Church and state.[35]

The Court then editorialized in an effort to explain its decision: A union of government and religion tends to destroy government and to degrade religion.[36]

Our founding fathers did not agree with such notions. In fact, George Washington said, "True religion affords to government its surest support." [37]

The Court reveals its contempt for the founding fathers in its continuing remarks:

It is true that New York's...prayer...does not amount to a total establishment of one particular religious sect to the exclusion of all others...That prayer seems relatively insignificant when compared to the governmental encroachment upon religion which were common place 200 years ago.[38]

The philosophical bent of this opinion and the attitude of the Court is clearly conveyed by its reasoning. The Court concluded that the founding fathers were violating the Constitution by their many religious references and practices. The arrogance of the Court is profound when you consider that members of the Court may be pretending to know more about what the Constitution meant than those who wrote it. The Scripture is again validated by the deeds of those who deny its relevance: "Although they claimed to be wise, they became fools" (Romans 1:22).

From this one illicit ruling, a series of godless decisions, aimed at destroying America's Christian heritage and removing the pillars of religion from the nation, ensued. Historically, court decisions have referred to previous cases as precedents to a new ruling, adding credibility and connectualism to past decisions. Exceptions to tradition are rare, however, in the case of *Engel v. Vitale*, the brief provided an outline that would make children who dared to pray in a classroom "law breakers." Not one single precedent was cited. Why? Because there was none!

How did the Court justify this illogic? They said: "These principles (of separation of Church and state) were so universally recognized." [39]

Referring to the *Engel v. Vitale* ruling as support for a subsequent decision, the courts simply said, in effect, "Everybody knows this is right." With that statement, the will of the people, the legislative process, and over two hundred years of practice in American life was overturned by the Supreme Court of the United States of America, and a new, destructive march toward moral relativism began.

Answered Prayer

When you examine closely the seemingly innocuous contents of the prayer that was struck down in the *Engel v. Vitale* decision of 1962, it is frightening how the prayer of the Supreme Court has been answered. The children were praying "Almighty God, we acknowledge our dependence upon Thee and we beg Thy blessings upon..."

1) "...Us" - Since 1962 our children have been victimized by broken homes, an explosion of sexual and physical abuse, the drug epidemic, gang violence, plummeting test scores, etc.

2) "...Our Parents" - Since 1962, their parents have seen their income eroded by burdensome taxes, exhaustive regulations and inflation, their marriages fail, their lives disrupted by a crime explosion, their physical health jeopardized by stress-related diseases and an epidemic of mental and emotional disorders, etc.

3) "...Our Teachers" - Since 1962, teachers have found themselves losing control of their classrooms due to the growing criminal activities of many students, the loss of respect once afforded their profession, and the growing responsibility of being called upon to both educate and

socialize children who enter school with no moral base.

4) "...Our Nation" - Since 1962, America has become a debtor nation with a deficit out of control. We now lead the world with more citizens in our prisons, more citizens on welfare, more illegitimate births, more divorces and more violent crime than any other nation on earth. Alexis de Tocqueville's observation has come true: "America is great because America is good. **If America ever ceases to be good, America will cease to be great**" (emphasis added).

It appears that the agonizing irony of the Supreme Court's landmark decision of 1962 is that it has proven that God answers prayer, and as we shall demonstrate, in the next chapter, He stopped blessing "us, our parents, our teachers and our nation" when an arrogant and illegitimate court demanded that our nation's children stop praying for it.

The Separation of Church and State is a Lie

The tragedy of our nation's plight is that it proceeded from a lie. Satan, who engineered the philosophical foundation of the atheistic communist regimes that kept one-third of the world's population in darkness for over seventy years, is the father of the lie. Jesus said that Satan is a liar and the father of all lies. When the Supreme Court Justices ruled that the Constitution erected a "wall of separation" between Church and state, they lied. Whether their actions were intentionally designed to subvert the truth or they acted in ignorance of the truth, is beside the point. The framers of our Constitution never erected such a wall. In fact, we have demonstrated, they saw the necessity for a union to exist between the Church and state, without which there could be no morality. John Adams wrote:

> Our Constitution was made only for a moral and religious people. It is wholly inadequate to the government of any other.[40]

David Barton, in his book, *The Myth of Separation,* thoroughly exposes the myth of the "wall of Church and state" logic. The First Amendment makes no such claim, simply stating:

> Congress shall make no law respecting an establishment of religion, or prohibiting the free exercise thereof, or abridging the freedom of speech, or of the press; or the right of the people peaceably to assemble and to petition the government for a redress or grievances.[41]

Recent judicial debates have revolved around the definition of what constitutes religion. The historical record proves the framers viewed religion and denomination as interchangeable words. In Europe, state churches funded by the government, had fallen victim to a corrupt clergy and religious intolerance. The framers of the Constitution were guarding against the danger of the federal government attempting to sponsor a national denomination. In America, there would be no state church.

A principle of propaganda is that any lie, no matter how absurd, if repeated enough, becomes believable. Today, "separation of Church and state" is believed to be a direct quote from the First Amendment. In fact, it is a rather obscure phrase from a letter written by Thomas Jefferson on January 1, 1802, in response to a letter from the Danbury Baptist Association, Danbury, Connecticut. In their letter to Jefferson, they expressed their concern for a rumor being circulated that a particular denomination was about to be recognized as the national denomination. Jefferson calmed their fears by writing:

> I contemplate with solemn reverence that act of the whole American people which declared that their legislature should 'make no law respecting the establishment of religion, or prohibiting the free exercise thereof', thus **building a wall of separation between Church and state**[42]

Jefferson was writing a personal letter to a group of concerned Baptists, assuring them America was not about to have a "Church of the United States." Ironically, those whose purpose has been to protect our children from the God they deny exists, have resorted to extracting eight words from a private correspondence. They were written by a man who was in France, serving as the U.S. Minister to France, throughout the time of the Constitutional Convention in 1787 and the drafting of the Bill of Rights in 1789. They had to bypass all of the participants in the Constitutional Convention, and every member of Congress who authored the First Amendment, to find someone who had written a letter from which they could extract favorable language to make their case. These facts are a moral outrage to our nation, and the resulting moral morass, apart from God's intervention, may be irreversible. Our only hope is found in God's promise:

> "If my people, who are called by my name will humble themselves and pray and seek my face and turn from their wicked ways, then

will I hear from heaven and will forgive their sin and will heal their land" (II Chronicles 7:14).

One Lie Gave Birth to Many Lies

The beginning of the dismantling of the "indispensable supports" of our society, morality and religion, referred to by President George Washington in his Farewell Address, was the 1947 *Everson* case. In that case, the Supreme Court first referred to a separation of Church and state in the First Amendment.

Following that announcement, the Court began systematically unraveling the American way of life.

In effect, one pillar of support was toppled, not by a consensus of the American people, but by the stroke of a Justice's pen. What a Great Depression, the Civil War and two World Wars could not do, A Supreme Court decision accomplished. Since 1947, the courts have decreed:

- A verbal prayer offered in a school is unconstitutional, even if it is both denominationally neutral and voluntarily participated in. *Engel v. Vitale,* 1962; *Abington v. Schempp,* 1963; *Commissioner of Ed. v. School Committee of Leyden,* 1971.

- Freedom of speech and press is guaranteed to students unless the topic is religious, at which time such speech becomes unconstitutional. *Stein v. Oshinsky,* 1965; *Collins v. Chandler Unified School Dist.,* 1981.

- If a student prays over his lunch, it is unconstitutional for him to pray aloud. *Reed v. Van Hoven,* 1965.

- It is unconstitutional for kindergarten students to say: "We thank you for the flowers so sweet; We thank you for the food we eat; We thank you for the birds that sing; We thank you for everything." Even though the word "God" is not contained in it, someone might think it is a prayer. *DeSpain v. DeKalb County Community School Dist.,* 1967.

- It is unconstitutional for a war memorial to be erected in the shape of a cross. *Lowe v. City of Eugene,* 1969.

- It is unconstitutional for students to arrive at school early to hear a student volunteer read prayers which had been offered by the chaplains in the chambers of the United States House of Representatives and Senate, even though those prayers are contained in the public Congressional Record published by the U.S. Government. *State Bd. of Ed. v. Board of Ed. of Netcong,* 1970.

- It is unconstitutional for a board of education to use or refer to the word "God" in any of its official writings. *State v. Whisner,* 1976.

- It is unconstitutional for a kindergarten class to ask, during a school assembly, whose birthday is celebrated at Christmas. *Florey v. Sioux Falls School Dist.,* 1979.

- It is unconstitutional for the Ten Commandments to hang on the walls of a classroom since it might lead the students to read them, meditate upon them, respect them, or obey them. *Sonte v. Graham,* 1980; *Ring v. Grand Forks Public School Dist.,* 1980; *Lanner v. Wimmer,* 1981.

- A bill becomes unconstitutional, even though the wording may be constitutionally acceptable, if the legislator who introduced the bill had a religious activity in his mind when he authored it. *Wallace v. Jaffree,* 1984.

- It is unconstitutional for a kindergarten class to recite: "God is great, God is good, let us thank Him for our food." *Wallace v. Jaffree,* 1984

- It is unconstitutional for a school graduation ceremony to contain an opening or closing prayer. *Graham v. Central Community School Dist.,* 1985; *Disselgrett v. Douglas School Dist.,* 1986.

- In the Alaska public schools [in 1987], students were told that they could not use the word "Christmas" in school because it had the word "Christ" in it. They were told that they could not have the word "Christmas" in their notebooks, or exchange traditional Christmas cards or presents, or even display anything with the word "Christmas" on it.

- In Virginia, a federal court has ruled that a homosexual newspaper may be distributed on a high school campus, but religious newspapers may not.

- Recently, public schools were barred from showing a film about the settlement of Jamestown, because the film depicted the erection of a cross at the settlement [despite the truth that] according to historical facts, a cross was erected at the Jamestown settlement...

- In 1987, a 185-year-old symbol of a Nevada city had to be changed because of its "religious significance,"...and a fire station was forced to remove a cross, a Christian symbol, which was placed there in remembrance of a fellow fireman who lost his life in the line of duty.

- In December of 1988, an elementary school principal in Denver removed the Bible from the school library and an elementary school music teacher in Colorado Springs stopped teaching Christmas carols because of alleged violations of the separation of Church and state.

- In Omaha, Nebraska, 10-year-old James Gierke was prohibited from reading his Bible silently during free time...the boy was forbidden by his teacher to open his Bible at school and was told doing so was against the law. [43]

George Washington warned us, in his Farewell Address, to "with caution indulge the supposition, that morality can be maintained without religion." The historical backdrop of his address was the French Revolution, where the churches were being burned and those who refused to be silent about their faith were being led to the guillotine. The streets of France ran red with blood as the pillar of religion was replaced by the sinking sand of religion. Morality was soon a matter of changing men's opinion.

James Kent was the Chief Justice of the Supreme Court of New York. Though he came along a few years later, he is considered the premier jurist in the development of the legal practice in the U.S. and authored the *Commentaries on American Law*. In 1811, he ruled on the guilt of a man whose crime was blaspheming Jesus Christ. Read the opinion of the Court, which he rendered:

The defendant was indicted...in December, 1810, for that he did, on the second day of September, 1810...wickedly, maliciously, and blasphemously, utter, and with a loud voice publish, in the presence and hearing of divers good and Christian people, of and concerning the Christian religion, and of and concerning Jesus Christ, the false, scandalous, malicious, wicked and blasphemous words following: "Jesus Christ was a bastard, and his mother must be whore," in contempt of the Christian religion...the defendant was tried and found guilty, and was sentenced by the court to be imprisoned for three months, and to pay a fine of $500.[44]

I wonder how Justice Kent would respond to today's "gangsta rap" and "heavy metal" music lyrics that glorify sex, violence, and even devil worship. I wonder how he would view the pornography that is unendingly rolling off the nation's presses in the name of free speech? Today, we fund, with our tax dollars, artists who do far more than utter that Jesus Christ was a bastard. Robert Mapplethorpe urinated in a jar and dropped a crucifix in upside down and called it "Piss Christ." For doing this in our enlightened age of no restraint, he received federal dollars through the National Endowment for the Arts. We've come a long way, haven't we!

Today's justices will not even allow public teachers to teach remedial classes if the classes meet in a parochial school, impeding a congressional mandate passed in 1965 to provide compensatory services to all needy students, regardless of where they attend school. (See: *Aguilar v. Felton* 1965.)

Christian brothers, we must endeavor to restore God to His rightful place in our nation, as militantly and methodically as the anti-God humanists and secularists have removed Him from the marketplace of ideas. They have effectively used the weapons of deceit and falsehood. We have the greater weapons of truth and persistence. Asserting our faith and our loyalty to God and His Word will not be popular, but the alternative is to forfeit our freedoms and resign our children to the tyranny of a world without hope. "Rise up, O men of God!" Let us arm ourselves with truth and restore our nation to her Christian heritage. "Enough is Enough!"

"Only a virtuous people are capable of freedom. As nations become corrupt and vicious, they have more need of masters."

-Benjamin Franklin - April 17, 1787

Chapter Seven

Statistics Don't Lie:
The Hedge Is Down

The hedge that once protected this nation is now all but gone. God is still restraining Satan in America today, but Pandora's Box has been opened. Evil now runs throughout America almost without check. I am eternally amazed that the leading thinkers and opinion makers of our day cannot seem to arrive at a consensus that anything is wrong. Two hundred thousand homosexuals and lesbians can converge on our capital, shout obscenities too vulgar to be reprinted, perform sex acts in public and have a female speaker shout her desire to "make it with Hillary" over the P.A., and it's celebrated as a victory for Gay Rights. In fact, the only wrong in today's culture is for a man of God to condemn such activity. We, as God's people, must remember that Almighty God is a witness to this wickedness.

The Disturbing Facts

All of the graphs that follow were compiled by William Bennett as he traces the decline of morality in America in his book, *The Index of Leading Cultural Indicators.* He tracks the growth of federal spending on various social programs that were designed to improve the quality of life for Americans and correct social evils. In the past thirty years, federal spending has increased over 600 billion dollars, measured in constant 1990 dollars, yet there was a 560 percent increase in violent crime, 400 percent increase in illegitimate births, a quadrupling in divorces, a tripling of the percentage of children living in single-parent-homes and a 200 percent increase in teenage suicides. During the same period, approximately 31,000,000 legal abortions were performed and SAT test scores plummeted an average of over 80 points. [46] America is clearly in a free-fall, morally. It is up to God's people like you and me to restore America to her Christian heritage.

America's humanist elite deny the existence of God and refuse to believe that religion has a role to play in encouraging moral values. They continue to believe that money and carefully crafted social programs are America's hope. As the graphs and statistics beginning on page 93 clearly reflect, the social programs of secular humanism do not work.

Alexander Solzhenitsyn, the Russian dissident who spent years in a Russian Gulag, writes, "The West has been undergoing an erosion and obscuring of high moral and ethical ideas. The spiritual axis of life has grown dim." [46]

William Bennett writes in the preface of his book, *The Devaluing of America*, these poignant words:

> The Scripture teaches people of faith two important lessons that we would do well to keep in mind in this modern age. The first is not to "grow weary or lose heart" in doing good. Righteousness is its own reward. The second is that although we are pilgrims and sojourners in this earthly kingdom, we are citizens of the city of God. Our growing optimism then has nothing to do with emerging victorious in the political battles in this world. "For here we do not have a lasting city, but we are seeking the city which is to come," the book of Hebrews reminds us. [47]

I have devoted the entire second section of this book to the death of the American dream and the birth of the American nightmare. I'd like to close this section by allowing you to see unmistakably that the supposition that America could have morality without religion was false. The lie of separation ushered in the moral collapse that is now being illustrated statistically. The sin of silence committed by millions of well intentioned people of faith has allowed the collapse to continue. If we are ever going to let our voice be heard, now is the time. The following graphs and charts compiled by William Bennett are detailed in his book, *The Leading Cultural Indicators*. David Barton details much of the same information in his book, *America, To Pray Or Not To Pray*.

Jerry Muller, who teaches modern European history at the Catholic

· Since 1965, the juvenile arrest rate for violent crimes has tripled.

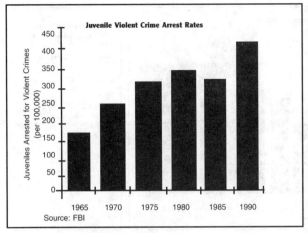

Year	Arrest Rate (per 100,000
1960	NA
1965	137.0
1970	215.9
1975	272.4
1980	338.1
1985	308.6
1990	430.6

Juvenile Violent Crime Arrest Rates

Source: FBI

· Since 1960, illegitimate birth rates have increased more than 400 percent.

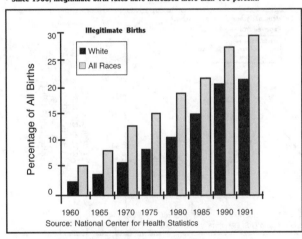

Illegitimate Births

Year	Percent White	Percent All Races
1960	2.3	5.3
1965	4.0	7.7
1970	5.7	10.7
1975	7.3	14.2
1980	11.0	18.4
1985	14.5	22.0
1990	21.0	28.0
1991	21.8	29.5

Source: National Center for Health Statistics

· The rate of births to unmarried teenagers has increased almost 200 percent since 1960.

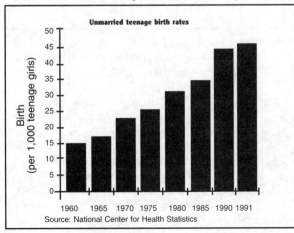

Unmarried teenage birth rates

Year	Rate (per 1,000 teenage girls)
1960	15.3
1965	16.7
1970	22.4
1975	23.9
1980	27.6
1985	31.6
1990	42.5
1991	44.8

Source: National Center for Health Statistics

· Since 1960, total crimes have increased by more than 300 percent.

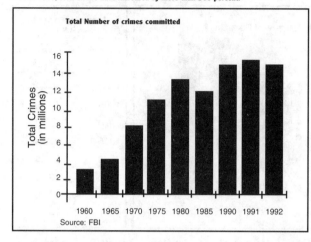

Total Number of crimes committed

Year	Total Crimes
1960	3,384,200
1965	4,739,400
1970	8,098,000
1975	11,292,400
1980	13,408,300
1985	12,431,400
1990	14,475,600
1991	14,872,900
1992	14,438,191

Source: FBI

· While expenditures on elementary and secondary education have increased more than 200 percent since 1960, SAT scores have declined 73 points.

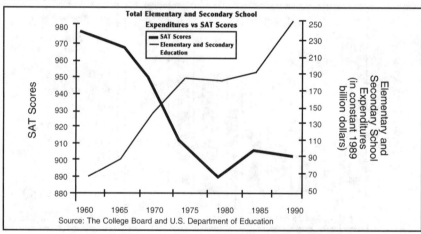

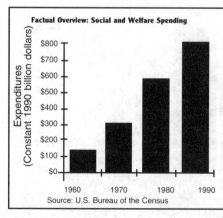

• Total social spending by the federal government, in constant 1990 dollars, has increased from $144 billion in 1960 to $787 billion in 1990.

• The percentage of social spending as part of America's Gross National Product has increased from 6.7 percent in 1960 to 14.4 percent in 1990.

• Federal expenditures on means-tested welfare programs have risen over 700 percent in the past 30 years, from $29 billion in 1960 to $212 billion in 1990 (in constant 1990 dollars).

94

University of America in Washington, D.C. wrote in "Commentary," February, 1991:

> If we had an Index of Leading Cultural Indicators, (now available, thanks to William Bennett), the level to which our popular culture has dropped might be charted by the fact that in the Summer and Autumn quarters of 1990, our dominant cultural elites were unable or unwilling to explain why the exhibitions of photographs of a man with a bullwhip up his anus (a Robert Mapplethorpe exhibit) should not be subsidized by the national government. Indeed, those who insisted that this was not an achievement worthy of collective support were angrily and contemptuously characterized by most of the cultural establishment as intellectual Neanderthals, too primitive to comprehend the nature of culture, which we were told must necessarily be committed to the exploration of new areas of experience. This reveals a deficit of moral resources far deeper and more troubling than our more noted budget and trade deficits.

Gentlemen, our forefathers were men of courage, confidence, and conviction. They grew tired of trying to appease a tyrant who was never content with what he had already taken from them. After years of trying to negotiate, the colonists decided to conduct a full-scale rebellion and either throw off the wicked rule of Great Britain or die trying. On July 4, 1776, fifty six men signed their own death warrants as they signed the "Declaration of Independence" from England. At the same time, they declared their total dependence on God, and God guided America to victory.

We too are at war. Our enemy is Satan. He is the same vile author of evil who first led a rebellion against God in the heavens and failed. Our weapons are not fleshly, but mighty through God, and we can win America back if we will unite around the cross, acknowledge our dependence on the "Captain of the Hosts" and then boldly confront the enemy. Faith always prevails over evil if and when we are willing to stand up and shout, "Enough is Enough!"

Remember, "for everyone born of God overcomes the world. This is the victory that has overcome the world, even our faith" (I John 5:4).

SECTION TWO

The Hedge Is Removed As The American Dream Fades

Introduction

"Stop trusting the man who has but a breath in his nostrils. Of what account is he? See now the Lord, the Lord Almighty is about to take from Jerusalem and Judah both supply and support" (Isaiah 2:22).

When I consider how much America has changed since the fifties and then try to project what America will be like forty years from now, I am overwhelmed with grief. Something tragically wrong is happening in our nation. Even the most liberal of our society recognizes that America cannot continue down the path she is on and survive. "Fixing America" has become the standard campaign rhetoric of every aspiring politician, yet nothing ever changes. The deficits get bigger, the new prisons are quickly filled, marriages continue to fail, more factories close and more lives are lost every day, every month and every year. What has happened to America?

Since the beginning, there have been two competing world views, vying for the control of American thought. These two world views have their origins in the God of Scripture and the god of this world. One is the God of truth and the other is the god of falsehood and deceit. Until the early sixties in this nation, the traditional Judeo-Christian ethic, rooted in the scripture, dominated the classrooms, the boardrooms and the courtrooms. Beginning in 1962, all that changed. The courts began to systematically secularize the nation, reflecting its view that God and the Scripture had no place in the public arena.

Two sins were committed. First, the United States Supreme Court, backed by the authority of the Federal Government, said in effect, "God has no place here." Secondly, the Church, comprised of tens of millions of Bible-believing Christians, failed to stand up and challenge this ungodly notion because they were too busy to get involved. Like the infamous "frog in kettle" analogy, Christians began swimming slowly in the increasingly hot water of secular humanism, choosing to adjust to each new anti-God ruling without much more than an occasional objection. Finally, we found ourselves in a boiling pot of secular humanism and our Judeo-Christian ethic, all but dead.

I believe America's pastors will have to answer to God if America is not restored. Alexis de Tocqueville said of his visit to America in the 1830's: "Not until I went into the churches of America and heard her pulpits flame with righteousness did I understand the secret of her genius and power." He went on to observe: "America is great because America

97

is good, and if America ever ceases to be good, America will cease to be great." [48] For more than a century, preachers of every persuasion have jointly looked to those words with understandable satisfaction and pride. Integrity now demands that we look at America's decline with corresponding shame and embarrassment. Where is the thundering, undaunted and united voice against the great sins of our culture? It is to our disgrace that the gay and lesbian communities hold greater influence over our legislative bodies, both locally and nationally, than does the Church. It is an indictment of the Church that we have now witnessed the slaughter of more than 35 million preborn boys and girls, and that their developing bodies are being used for scientific research in laboratories across America. There are some voices crying out against the darkness that is engulfing America. Perhaps the clearest voice is Dr. James Dobson, a layman and son of a preacher.

He is not alone. Men like Jerry Falwell, D. James Kennedy, Pat Robertson, Tim LaHaye and Chuck Colson are attempting to awaken the American Christian conscience to say "Enough is Enough." These men may not agree on every theological point of doctrine, but these are men who are speaking openly about sin. There are thousands of other lesser known and unknown, but faithful, preachers of the infallible Word of God who daily take their stand across America in small towns and communities. Preachers must again ignite their pulpits with the flame of righteousness if America shall be restored. The greatest hope for the nation is the local New Testament Church, aflame with the truth.

Not only will God hold preachers accountable, He will hold laymen accountable as well. Many preachers have attempted to take a stand against sin in their community, only to have the platform from which they spoke jerked out from under them by a carnal congregation. Carnal laypeople have refused to give God his ten percent in the form of a tithe, often limiting the ability of the church to perform meaningful ministry for lack of funds. Now these same laypeople find themselves being compelled to give as high as forty to fifty percent of their income through various forms of taxation. Instead of the church compassionately meeting the needs of people in the name of Christ through freewill offerings, we now have professional bureaucrats doling out confiscated money, without compassion, to people who are largely unaccountable to anyone, in an ever increasing welfare state that is bankrupt, both financially and morally. If I give my money to the poor, that is compassion. If I give your money to the poor, that is theft. Politicians have made careers out of confiscating the money of law-abiding citizens through exorbitant taxation and in turn legitimizing unscriptural behavior with countless government subsidies.

In the following nine chapters, we are going to see what the Prophet Isaiah predicted would happen to Jerusalem and Judah if God removed the hedge He had established around the nation. In Section One we discussed "The Hedge Is Raised: As The American Dream Is Born." Next, we are going to discuss "The Hedge Is Removed: As The American Dream Fades." My heart aches as I consider how far we have fallen from the vision of our founders.

In 1962, the highest court of our nation said to school children that they could not pray "Almighty God, we acknowledge our dependence upon Thee...." Careful study of the curriculum taught in our schools today reveals that we encourage our children to trust in man, but we forbid them to publicly acknowledge their trust in God. Through a careful and diligent process, most references to the historic faith of our founders has been excluded from our children's textbooks in public education. The theory of evolution is taught as fact, encouraging our children to believe that they are nothing more than a small part of the evolutionary process. For three decades, students have been taught the lie that they are simply animals, nothing more. Now that they are acting like animals, everyone is asking, "Why?"

The process of teaching Creation Science is looked upon with contempt by many within the educational establishment. The American Civil Liberties Union has prosecuted countless school districts that dared to give children a biblical balance to the theory of evolution on the grounds that it defies the First Amendment. For the same reason, they have refused to allow school districts to teach abstinence when the matter of sex education was discussed. With the same rationale, the courts even ruled the Ten Commandments could not be posted on the walls of a public building. In the *Stone v. Graham* ruling of 1980, the Supreme Court ruled it unconstitutional to hang the Ten Commandments on the walls of a classroom, since, as they reasoned, it might lead the students to read them, meditate upon them, respect them or obey them.

Since 1962, we have witnessed one bizarre ruling after another flow forth from the courts of our land as the elite of our nation have begun to apply their worldview that eliminates God from the equation and makes man the savior of himself.

The Tenets of Secular Humanism

In 1980, Tim LaHaye published a 247 page book entitled *The Battle*

For The Mind. More than anything I have read on the subject, this book opened my eyes to the tenets of secular humanism and the grip that this wicked philosophy has held on American education since the 1930's. In the book he writes:

> Humanism appeals to the intellect and intelligent people tend to be largely of the melancholy temperament. Although endowed with great talent and creativity, (they) are apt to be idealistic, theoretical and impractical, making them vulnerable to humanistic philosophy, even though it has a long history of disorder, anguish and despair.[49]

The *Humanist Manifesto I* was published in the 1930's and signed by a host of thirty-four liberal humanists including none other than John Dewey, known as the Father of Modern American Education. It is the bible of secular humanism. In 1973, an updated edition was published entitled *Humanist Manifesto II.* The "Manifesto" proclaims itself a "positive declaration for times of uncertainty." Dr. LaHaye presents the following quotes from the *Humanist Manifesto II* that affirms their belief in the five basic tenets of humanism:

Tenet I: Atheism

"Religious humanists regard the universe as self-existing and not created...We find insufficient evidence for belief in the existence of a supernatural; it is either meaningless or irrelevant to the question of the survival and fulfillment of the human race. As nontheists, we begin with humans, not God, nature, not deity. Nature may indeed be broader and deeper than we now know; any new discoveries, however, will but enlarge our knowledge of the natural...But we can discover no divine purpose or providence for the human species. While there is much that we do not know, humans are responsible for what we are or will become. No deity will save us, we must save ourselves."

Tenet II: Evolution

"Humanism believes that man is part of nature and that he has emerged as the result of a continuous process...Holding an organic view of life, humanists find that the traditional dualism of mind and body must be rejected...Humanism recognizes that man's religious culture and civilization, as clearly depicted by anthropology and history, are the product of a gradual development due to his interaction with his natural environment and with his social heritage. The individual born into a particular culture is largely molded to that culture...science affirms that the human species is an emergence from natural evolutionary forces. As far as we know, the total personality is a function of the biological organism transacting in a social and cultural context. There is no credible evidence that life survives the death of the body. We continue to exist in our progeny and in the way that our lives have influenced others in our culture."

Tenet III: Amorality

"We affirm that moral values derive their source from human experience. Ethics is autonomous and situational, needing no theological or ideological sanction. Ethics stems from human need and interest. To deny this distorts the whole basis of life. In the area of sexuality, we believe that intolerant attitudes, often cultivated by orthodox religions and puritanical cultures, unduly repress sexual conduct. The right to birth control, abortion, and divorce should be recognized. While we do not approve of exploitative, denigrating forms of sexual expression, neither do we wish to prohibit, by law or social sanction, sexual behavior between consenting adults. The many varieties of sexual exploration should not in themselves be considered "evil." Without countenancing mindless permissiveness or unbridled promiscuity, a civilized society should be a tolerant one. Short of harming others or compelling them to do likewise, individuals should be permitted to express their sexual proclivities and pursue their life-styles as they desire. We wish to cultivate the development of a responsible attitude toward sexuality, in which humans are not exploited as sexual objects, and in which intimacy, sensitivity, respect, and honesty in interpersonal relations are encouraged. Moral education for children and adults is an important way of developing awareness and sexual maturity." (Morality devoid of biblical values. Author's note.)

Tenet IV: Individual Autonomy

"Human life has meaning because we create and develop our futures. Happiness and the creative realization of human needs and desires, individually and in shared enjoyment, are continuous themes of humanism. We strive for the good life, here and now. The goal is to pursue life's enrichment despite debasing forces of vulgarization, commercialization, bureaucratization, and dehumanization...Reason and intelligence are the most effective instruments that humankind possesses. There is no substitute: neither faith nor passion suffices in itself. The controlled use of scientific methods, which have transformed the natural and social sciences since the Renaissance, must be extended further in the solution of human problems...To enhance freedom and dignity the individual must experience a full range of civil liberties in all societies. This includes freedom of speech and the press, political democracy, the legal right of opposition to governmental policies, fair judicial process, religious liberty, freedom of association, and artistic, scientific, and cultural freedom. It also includes a recognition of an individual's right to die with dignity, euthanasia, and the right to suicide.

"We oppose the increasing invasion of privacy, by whatever means, in both totalitarian and democratic societies. We would safeguard, extend, and implement the principles of human freedom evolved from the *Magna Carta* to the *Bill of Rights*, the *Rights of Man*, and the *Universal Declaration of Human Rights*...The preciousness and dignity of the individual person is a central humanist value. Individuals should be encouraged to realize their own creative talents and desires. We reject all religious, ideological, or moral codes that denigrate the individual, suppress freedom, dull intellect, dehumanize personality. We believe in maximum individual autonomy consonant with social responsibility. Although science can account for the causes of behavior, the possibilities of individual freedom of choice exist in human life and should be increased."

Tenet V: Socialistic One-World View
"We deplore the division of humankind on nationalistic grounds. We have reached a turning point in human history where the best option is to transcend the limits of national sovereignty and to move toward the building of a world community in which all sectors of the human family can participate. Thus we look to the development of a system of world law and a world order based upon transnational federal government. This would appreciate cultural pluralism and diversity. It would not exclude pride in national origins and accomplishments nor the handling of regional problems on a regional basis. Human progress, however, can no longer be achieved by focusing on one section of the world, Western or Eastern, developed or underdeveloped. For the first time in human history, no part of humankind can be isolated from any other. Each person's future is in some way linked to all. We thus reaffirm a commitment to the building of world community, at the same time recognizing that this commits us to some hard choices...The problems

of economic growth and development can no longer be resolved by one nation alone; they are worldwide in scope. It is the moral obligation of the developed nations to provide - through an international authority that safeguards human rights - massive technical, agricultural, medical, and economic assistance, including birth control techniques, to the developing portions of the globe. World poverty must cease. Hence extreme disproportions in wealth, income, and economic growth should be reduced on a worldwide basis.

"The principle of moral equality must be furthered through elimination of all discrimination based upon race, religion, sex, age, or national origin. This means equality of opportunity and recognition of talent and merit. Individuals should be encouraged to contribute to their own betterment. If unable, then society should provide means to satisfy their basic economic, health, and cultural needs, including, wherever resources make possible, a minimum guaranteed annual income." [50]

Tim LaHaye Summarizes:

Atheism: "We find insufficient evidence for belief in the existence of the supernatural...as nontheists we begin with man not God...no deity will save us; we must save ourselves."

Evolution: "Religious Humanists regard the universe as self-existing and not created...the human species is an emergence from natural evolutionary forces."

Amorality: "Ethics is autonomous and situational ...and stem from self interest - favor right to birth control, abortion, divorce and choice of sex direction."

Individual Autonomy: "We believe in maximum individual autonomy - reject all religious, moral codes that suppress freedom...demand civil liberties, including right to oppose governmental policies - right to die with dignity, euthanasia and suicide."

Socialist One-World View: "We have reached a turning point in human history where the best often is to transcend the limits of national sovereignty and move toward the building of a world community...the peaceful adjudication of differences by international courts." [51]

Can there be any doubt as we approach the 21st Century that

humanism is the dominant philosophy of American thought today? We may still exalt the God of Scripture in our church buildings, but the religion of secular humanism is driving public policy. Isaiah's prophecy takes an ominous tone:

> "Stop trusting in man...see now, the Lord, the LORD Almighty, is about to take from Jerusalem and Judah both supply and support" (Isaiah 2:22 3:1).

My deeply held conviction that the scripture is God-breathed and completely inspired compels me to believe that even the order in which the revelation of Isaiah 3 is given has significance. As Isaiah delivers this prophetic word to a nation that forgets God, there is a growing release of evil, each with progressively more tragic consequences than the one preceding.

In the following material, you will see the devastating consequences that befall a nation as it embraces more and more of the humanist philosophy and drifts increasingly away from God and His revelation.

"I fear for our nation. Nearly half of our people receive some form of government subsidy. We have grown weak from too much affluence and too little adversity. I fear that soon we will not be able to defend our country from our sure and certain enemies. We have debased our currency to the point that even the most loyal citizen no longer trusts it."

- Roman Senator AD 63 [52]

Chapter Eight

A Faltering Economy

"See now, the Lord, the Lord Almighty, is about to take from Jerusalem and Judah...all supplies of food and all supplies of water" (Isaiah 3:1).

In the ancient world of Isaiah's Judah, life was often reduced to having the basic two necessities of life: food and water. In the arid climate of the Middle East, if the water was withheld, the food was soon lost. Again and again, throughout the nation's history, God used drought to punish the nation's sin.

The prophet announced that God would withhold the supplies of food and water from the nation for the sin of turning from the living God and putting their trust in man. In 20th Century American life, things are not so simple. Our great and benevolent God graced America unlike any nation in all of world history. Protected by vast oceans to the East and West, He provided natural barriers to invading armies. He then laid vast reservoirs of oil and gas beneath the surface of the soil, not to mention coal and other mineral resources. Over the years, these incredible treasures have provided untold wealth to our citizens and national treasury as God granted abundant prosperity (Deuteronomy 28:11). Add to that the gold and silver that He laid inside her mountains, rich soil in the farm belt that enabled America to feed the world (Deuteronomy 28:8), incredibly fertile meadows on which to graze our livestock (Deuteronomy 28:4), pure streams and rivers that feed our bountiful lakes, brimming with fish and providing safe haven to our multitudes of waterfowl, and the lush forests, alive with game and rich in timber. How fitting are the words of Isaiah, "What more could have been done for my vineyard than I have done for it?" (Isaiah 5:4).

Capitalizing on the nation's bountiful natural resources, the founding fathers developed a free-enterprise, capitalistic, economic system that rewarded diligence and risk-taking (faith). The most vibrant and prosperous economy the world has ever known was the result.

America Is Declared A Christian Nation

Debt was unknown in America, with the exception of periods of war. Even then, soon after every war, the debt that accumulated was quickly eliminated, because of the prosperity of the nation. America was a nation with a purpose. America was a nation with a God and He was the God of the Bible. Even the Supreme Court of 1892 recognized that America was a Christian nation. In the case of *Rector, etc., of the Holy Trinity Church v. United States*, February 29, 1892, the court ruled that, "the case assumes that we are a Christian country and the morality of the country is deeply engrafted upon Christianity...These and many other matters which might be noticed, add a volume of unofficial declarations to the mass of organic utterances that (America) is a Christian nation." But in spite of all God's blessings, it wasn't enough. As the courts began redefining the role of religion in America and systematically dethroning God, the people began to increasingly put their trust in man.

Today, the supplies of our vast economic system are being stripped away. History should be the master teacher of the present. Following America's shame of the slave trade came the devastation of the Civil War and the era of exploitation that followed. Following the debauchery of the "roaring '20s" with its open hedonism came the Great Depression. Following the willful tolerance of Adolph Hitler's ideology of aggression and anti-semitism came World War II. Why do we think we will escape the ultimate insult to God of removing Him and His Word from public policy? We have replaced Him, the Lord God Almighty, with empty secular humanism. We now have a generation of self-made gods who live for themselves, making up the rules as they go. Many today indulge every lustful appetite, caring for no one but themselves with no regard for God nor any other living thing, including the most defenseless of our society, the elderly and the unborn? Has He removed the supplies? I will let you be the judge.

Just one generation ago it was common place for a man to sign on for life with a company. Company loyalty was a two-way street. In exchange for being faithful to work hard and discharge your duties with propriety, you could be assured of permanent employment, good benefits, and an adequate retirement at age 65. My own father is an example of such company loyalty and is today enjoying the benefits. Today, manufacturing jobs have all but disappeared. Companies have either moved operations outside the country or ceased to operate, due to high labor costs, excessive taxes and endless litigation, often prompted by changing regulations and information made available years after the fact. The steel industry is a prime example of a supply being removed.

Two Disturbing Books By Larry Burkett

The economic base of this country is being eroded. Small business is being eliminated by government regulations. Christian economist Larry Burkett has written two frightening books that detail the morass that our economy is in; *The Coming Economic Earthquake* and *Whatever Happened to the American Dream*.

In *Whatever Happened to the American Dream*, Burkett describes eight factors converging on the American economy as this millennium draws to a close that could turn the American dream into an American nightmare. They are: (1) the aging United States population, (2) the declining youth population (caused in large measure by the abortion holocaust), (3) governmental regulations, (4) lower savings, (5) rising health care costs, (6) declining industry, (7) endless lawsuits, and (8) rising debt.

Burkett discusses in detail how the federal government has become god to many citizens. He states, "The federal government has evolved, by way of individual apathy, into being the great provider, protector and general all-around decision maker for the country." To illustrate the point, Burkett documents how the Occupational Safety and Health Administration (OSHA) and the Environmental Protection Agency (EPA) both shackle small businesses with endless regulations that often make the costs of doing business exorbitant. OSHA and the EPA have broad powers that exceed anything that the founding fathers ever imagined for the federal government. An audit by either agency can be ruinous to a small company, costing tens of thousands of dollars in lost revenues and wasted man-hours. One regulator, unaccountable to anyone, least of all the tax paying citizenry, has within his power the ability to destroy a small business. Yet in America, it is not "politically correct" to even question this authority. Just ask members of Congress who in the summer of 1995 recommended curtailing the power of the Federal Regulatory Agencies. The conservatives in Congress who dared to discuss this "Golden Calf," were accused by the liberal establishment of wanting to poison America's water, pollute America's air and annihi-late America's wildlife.

Today, OSHA employs approximately 35,000 regulators snooping around in the work place at a cost of tens of millions of dollars to American taxpayers and adding enormous expense to the cost of doing business in America. Burkett documents dozens of cases of abuse of small businesses at the hands of federal regulators, causing countless compa-nies to simply give up and/or move their operations out of the country. They make for interesting reading. NAFTA has made the lure to move to regulation-free Mexico extremely appealing. All the while, jobs are lost and the U.S. economy is eroding.

You may be thinking, as most Americans do, is not having a safe place to work a good thing? Of course it is, but what is often forgotten by our litigious society is that we do not live in a perfect world. No amount of regulation will ever result in an accident-free work place. Someone will always do something stupid. There will always be an accident. People who invest their life savings in a business have a right to expect a reasonable return on their investment. When their life's work is subject to being destroyed on the whims of a federal regulator who has the weight of the federal government behind him and an army of legal staff at his disposal, small businessmen finally lose the initiative to fight the system. Small business has been the genius of the American economic system, but that supply is being withdrawn with grave implications for the future.

The story of the EPA is even more disturbing. Everyone wants clean air and pure water, hence few will dare take on the EPA, but Burkett does a splendid job discussing the abuses of this federal agency. I would like to consider one constitutional right that our founding fathers fought to secure, that an employee of the EPA can take away from an American citizen without firing a shot. The Fifth Amendment to the U.S. Constitution submitted as part of our "Bill of Rights" states that: "no person...shall be deprived of life, liberty or property without due process of law; nor shall private property be taken for public use without just compensation." This right is trampled on daily in America. Just compensation is seldom, if ever, granted when investment property is rendered useless because a regulator discovers an obscure endangered species.

Our founding fathers fought for the right to own private property, a right few men enjoyed in the Old World. But today, under the high-flying banner of protecting "the public interest," the control of private property is often passing into the hands of federal regulators. Nightmare stories are endless of private citizens losing their fortunes and their dreams because a regulator declared their property to be wetlands, or the home to any one of hundreds of endangered species under the banner of the 1973 Endangered Species Act. This act has enabled a radical group of antibusiness environmentalists to stop development and punish landowners. In December of 1992, a U.S. District Judge approved the addition of 401 plant and animal species to the list by 1996, and another 900 later. [53] If the environmentalists have their way, an additional 3,000 species will be added in the near future. The spotted owl has become the national symbol of the radical extremists within the environmental movement and their power for economic disruption with the aid of federal regulators. They recently shut down eight-and-one-half million acres of public and private timberland that was declared spotted owl habitat. This action put hundreds of people out of work, impacting the cost of lumber, nationwide, and prevented private citizens from reaping the financial benefit of harvesting valuable timber on their own property.

Man Was Granted Dominion Over The Earth

The first recorded commandment in God's Word to man is found in Genesis 1:27-28:

> "So God created man in his own image, in the image of God he created him; male and female he created them. God blessed them and said to them, 'Be fruitful and increase in number; fill the earth and subdue it. Rule over the fish of the sea and the birds of the air and over every living creature that moves on the ground.'"

Man is not just another animal. He is a created being, made in the image of God. Unlike the lesser animals, God "breathed in his nostrils the breath of life and man became a living being" (Genesis 2:7). God fully intended man to rule over the earth and for every creature and plant to be subjected to him. That in no way gives man the right to wreck his environment nor wastefully destroy animal life. God gave specific rules and regulations designed to protect the environment from abuse in the Levitical Code.

The extremist environmentalists see man as just another animal competing with other animals for limited resources. The radical extremists see man as the problem and they are intent on destroying man's economic development.

Regarding the environment, Rush is right (Rush Limbaugh, that is)! He writes:

> The real enemies of the radical environmental leadership are capitalism and the American way of life.... The radical environmentalists believe "big government regulation" is the best way to protect the environment (and they) have adopted their cause with all of the fervor and enthusiasm of a religious crusade, abandoning reason and accepting many faulty premises on faith.[54]

Limbaugh cites an article that was published in the *New York Times* magazine on May 30, 1993, written by Harvard Professor Edward O. Wilson. The article entitled "Is Humanity Suicidal?" illustrates how far outside of mainstream America many in the environmental movement have drifted. He writes:

> Darwin's dice may have rolled badly for earth. It was a misfortune for the living world in particular, many scientists believe, that a carnivorous primate and not some more benign form of animal made the breakthrough. Our species retains hereditary traits that add greatly to our destructive impact.[55]

These words are an affront to a Holy God, yet they are written by a learned professor who teaches sociobiology to our next generation of leaders at Harvard. Harvard has come a long way since being established through the generosity of Rev. John Harvard. The declared purpose of the institution, established in 1636, was "to train a literate clergy."

In the "Rules and Precepts" of Harvard University, published in 1642, the second precept stated:

> Let every student be plainly instructed, and earnestly pressed to consider well, the main end of his life and studies is, to know God and Jesus Christ...the only foundation of all sound knowledge and learning.[56]

Isaiah warns the nation that refuses to honor God, choosing rather to trust man, that God will remove the supplies of food and the supplies of water. How much more can the U.S. economy absorb? Business must be prepared to endure endless threats of lawsuits, spiraling insurance costs, unknown economic factors like higher interest rates and inflation, excessive government regulations, ever-rising taxes, natural disasters, rising labor costs, and decreasing skills in the labor force. The federal government has become business' chief competitor for unskilled labor, rewarding welfare recipients by making it more financially attractive to remain jobless than to enter the job market at minimum wage. Why should anyone want to give up tax free income, free medical care, food stamps and aid for their dependent children, to work in the heat for a general contractor at minimum wage or at a fast food restaurant. The "Great Society" of Lyndon Johnson gave the false hope to millions of American citizens that the federal government was society's big brother. We now have tens of millions of citizens who are second and third generation welfare recipients. Grover Cleveland understood the danger of building a welfare state:

> I will not be a party to stealing money from one group of citizens to give to another group of citizens; no matter what the need or apparent justification. Once the coffers of the federal govern-ment are open to the public, there will be no shutting them again. It is the responsibility of the citizens to support their government. It is not the responsibility of the government to support its citizens.[57]

Karl Marx, the father of Communism and a contemporary of Grover Cleveland, wrote:

> A democracy is not a form of government to survive. For it will succeed until its citizens discover they can vote themselves money from the treasury, then they will bankrupt it.[58]

It appears that Karl Marx better understood human nature than do our politicians of today. Today, the federal government routinely confiscates money from one group of citizens and transfers the money to another, via farm supports, social security, welfare, aid to dependent children, various feeding programs, grants in aid for college students, etc. No one denies that the money is needed by many and even appreciated by most.

The fact remains the whole philosophy flies in the face of both Scripture and reason. Scripture again becomes relevant:

"Do not be deceived: God cannot be mocked. A man reaps what he sows. The one who sows to please his sinful nature, from that nature will reap destruction; the one who sows to please the Spirit, from the Spirit will reap eternal life" (Galatians 6:7-8)

Supplemental Security Income

John O'Donnell and Jim Haner recently authored a detailed account of how far some people go in this nation to "get their share" at taxpayers' expense. Their story was originally carried in the *Baltimore Sun*. I read their story in an issue of *The Mike Richards News Digest* in June of 1995. The focus of the article centered on a family in Lake Providence, Louisiana and how they tapped into a little known welfare program run by the Social Security Administration called Supplemental Security Income (SSI). It was originally established by Congress in 1974, for the purpose of providing life's necessities for poor adults who were too old, ill or handicapped to work. In 1995, its 6.3 million recipients included drug addicts, the mentally ill, the excessively obese and over 900,000 children who receive over 25 billion dollars annually. This most generous of all welfare plans has more than doubled in cost since 1990 and is expected to grow by over 50% over the next four years because the word is spreading on the streets.

The family in Lake Providence, Louisiana, as reported by O'Donnell and Haner, illustrate the abuse at your expense. The first applicant in the household was the mother. She applied five times over eleven years, because she understood the SSI benefits were more generous than traditional welfare. Her persistence paid off. Listing a different disability on each application (anemia, dizziness, etc.) in 1985 she was approved. By that time she had enlisted six of seven children and her common-law husband. Because SSI pays retroactive bonuses covering approved applicants back to the original application, the Lake Providence, Louisiana family has received over $36,000 in retroactive, tax-free bonuses. I have worked all my adult life and never received a bonus that even approached this tax-free gift. Of the bonuses I have received, I always paid the taxes required. Can a nation long exist that is so committed to defying the Scripture that teaches: "If a man will not work, he shall not eat" (2 Thessalonians 3:10)? A compassionate nation certainly should strive to assist the less fortunate among them, but, according to the report, this family receives a tax-free income of over $46,000 per year,[59] plus free medical treatment at unlimited potential to the taxpayers. Will we have to see the nation completely fall into bankruptcy before we stand up and say "Enough is Enough?" The eight recipients in this family of nine receive their tax-free money because one is "mildly retarded," one is "easily irritated, aggressive and explosive," one is "too obese," and one is simply "unable to work." Karl Marx was correct when he assessed that, "when citizens discover they can vote themselves money from the treasury, they will bankrupt it." In post Christian America, we are handing out money faster than hard working citizens can pay it in through excessive taxation.

The Growing National Debt

John F. Kennedy, in his inaugural speech said, "Ask not what your country can do for you...but rather what you can do for your country." At that time in 1961, there were approximately 22 million people on our welfare rolls nationwide. During President's Johnson's administration, the Vietnam War and his declared war on poverty at home created massive spending. Over a five year period, over 600 billion dollars was needed to fund his two declared wars. In seven years, from 1963 to 1970, federal income taxes increased by forty-two percent while incomes rose only twelve percent, and still revenues could not keep up with expenditures. The roller coaster ride was just beginning.

The total federal debt rose by 90 billion dollars from 1960 to 1970. It climbed by $600 billion from 1970 to 1980. By 1979, inflation was running at twelve percent per year. People began borrowing to hedge against inflation. They believed it was better to purchase now, on credit, than to wait a year to pay cash only to see the cost of an item rise an additional twelve percent. This lead to an explosion in personal credit spending while feeding the human desire for instant gratification. Today, personal savings are at an all-time low in America while personal debt is at an all-time high. Both are unhealthy signs. Few things put greater stress on a marriage and lead to more breakups than excessive debt.

How far have we come since John F. Kennedy's inaugural speech of 1961. In 1995, our Federal Government is so committed to the expansion of the welfare state and the redistribution of wealth, that they actually advertise for participants. These are books being produced and sold that teach people how to tap into government giveaway system. There is even a title for this new approach to recruitment called "Outreach." How tragic is the abuse of this term. In Christian circles, "Outreach" is the designation used to describe recruitment of new members for the church as they are encouraged to place their hope and faith in Christ, whom they are told, can and will meet their needs. Now the Federal Government is using the same term to in effect say, "Big Brother Government" will be your god.

In New York City alone, during the summer of 1995, more than $400,000 was expended for advertising to inform citizens that they could get "free" money. The New York Human Resource Aministration provides a 1-900 number that you can call and receive instructions on how to get enrolloed. America is clearly on a course of self destruction and financial collapse.

The federal debt is now approaching 5 trillion dollars and is still climbing at an alarming rate. To help illustrate how much money we are talking about, visualize that 5 trillion dollars, in tightly bound $1,000.00 bills, would produce a stack over 310 miles high. At some point in the not too distant future, if current trends continue unaborted, the day will come when the interest on the national debt will exceed the government income. A one or two point rise in the cost of borrowing money could accelerate that day significantly. The result would be an economic collapse making the Great Depression look like a day in the park. When that happens, Americans will see everything they've worked for taken away and they will not be able to secure the basic necessities of life. During the Great Depression era, most Americans had a deeply held faith in God to fall back on that produced great character and moral strength. At the height of the depression, crimes remained very low. I doubt that Americans today will respond in that fashion if America faces another collapse.

Larry Burkett traces the collapse of the German economic system. Following World War I, the Germans incurred great debt as a result of having to pay reparations to her European neighbors. Hyperinflation resulted in a valueless currency and the massive shift of assets to the wealthy. This effectively eliminated the middle class. Those events set the stage for Adolph Hitler, an ex-army corporal, who promised restored prosperity for all. If our economy collapsed today, American culture would be fertile soil for a political despot to rise to power, promising economic stability and law and order in the streets.

Natural Disasters

Before we leave this important subject of the economy and our growing inability to meet our most basic needs, a word about recent weather patterns and "acts of God" (insurance vernacular) is in order. In our modernistic, era of news reporting, no one dares to attempt to read into any of the recent catastrophic events of our nation any biblical significance, but I feel compelled to make a few observations.

Our nation has been racked by torrential rainfall, producing record flooding along the Mississippi River; mudslides, brushfires and earthquakes in California; tornadoes and violent weather in the Midwest; drought in the Southwest; and hurricanes along the coasts, including two of the costliest in history. The financial impact of these tragedies could not have come at a worse time. Add to these "acts of God;" the south-central Los Angeles riot, numerous ill-advised military operations like our recent excursion into Haiti; and the financial toll is staggering.

As our deficits have exploded, politicians have been reticent to mention still higher taxes, at least until our current President reversed his campaign promise to lower taxes and instead enacted one of the largest tax increases in history. Even then, he found it necessary to first invoke class envy, pitting the middle and poor classes against the rich, posturing himself as a friend of the working class. Ironically, the increased tax on gasoline impacted the working class the most, as gasoline prices have reached an all-time high, along with the increased cost of shipping and transporting, passed directly on to the consumers.

The High Cost of Gambling

The latest revenue-generating rage in America is gambling. Lotteries run by state officials, as well as the taxing of America's fastest growing industry, legalized gambling, has once again given our governmental agencies a vested interest in something God clearly hates. The whole premise of gambling is that man can get something for which he did not work. Gambling seeks to undermine the very judgment that Holy God placed on the sin of Adam and through Adam, the whole human race. God pronounced upon Adam:

> "Because you listened to your wife and ate from the tree about which I commanded you, 'You must not eat of it; cursed is the ground because of you; through painful toil you will eat of it all the days of your life'" (Genesis 3:17).

The gambling industry, driven by greed and corruption, spends billions of dollars in an attempt to convince potential customers that they have the chance to beat the system and gain untold wealth without painful toil. In these days of darkness, revenue-starved state governments are now taxing "ignorance" as often those who can least afford to squander their few hard earned dollars, become addicted to the false hope that they might be the next millionaire as they invest in lottery tickets.

Though the immediate sensation of huge amounts of cash flowing into state treasuries is intoxicating, certain terrible judgment awaits. With delayed payments, stretching out 20 years in the future, and amounting to enormous sums, we are obligating our children for the funding. At the same time we are creating even greater appetites for easy money as every dime received is spent without reducing existing deficits. Meanwhile, families are being destroyed by the demon of gambling.

In states like Mississippi, where the beautiful coastline has become polluted with Las Vegas-style casinos promising instantaneous gratification, family restaurants, and hotel establishments which have existed for years, employing hundreds of taxpaying, law abiding citizens, are being driven out of business. They simply cannot compete with discounted room rates and free or ridiculously inexpensive meals offered by the casinos. And why do the casinos give away so much? Because they know that if you check into their hotel, the odds are overwhelming that when you leave, you'll leave everything.

There are other businesses thriving on the Mississippi and Louisiana coastline. Along with the casinos is a thriving business in law enforcement and pawnshops. Time will tell if the temporary boom in tax revenues generated by the gambling industry will even offset the lost revenue of businesses that are being destroyed and the rising cost of law enforcement that always follows the casino crowd.

With the loss of the Judeo-Christian ethic that dominated American thought just forty years ago, a new morality has come which has enabled the unthinkable to become common. On more than one occasion, I have witnessed a single mother pull up to a "Stop 'n Go" type of establishment, leave three or four small children in a dilapidated car, rush in with a fistful of dollars and purchase an equal number of lottery tickets. My heart groans as she drives away a little more jaded, while her much-needed cash resources are transferred into the vast governmental treasury to be redistributed by professional politicians and bureaucrats. God be merciful to America!

"Young man, the secret of my success is that at an early age I discovered I was not God."

-Oliver Wendell Holmes - March 8, 1931
Associate Justice of the
U.S. Supreme Court
1902-1932

Chapter Nine

The Demise Of
America's Heroes

"See now, the Lord, the LORD Almighty, is about to take from Jerusalem and Judah both supply and support...the hero and warrior, the judge and prophet, the soothsayer and elder, the captain of fifty and man of rank, the counselor, skilled craftsman and clever enchanter" (Isaiah 3:1-3).

In Chapter Eight, we examined the removal of the supplies reflected in a faltering U.S. economy and discussed some of the reasons why it is failing. In this chapter, we shall explore America's loss of character and trace how it effects such diverse institutions as the military and the courts. There was a day, not so long ago, when a man's word was his bond. For decades in America, legal contracts were mere formalities, and in many cases, nonexistent. Millions of dollars transferred hands based on a simple handshake.

In today's world, it is often said in the business community, that a contract is worth no more than the paper on which it is written. Attorney's fees are considered part of the cost of doing business, as exacting language is carefully penned in an effort to force people to keep their commitment. Integrity and character are in short supply.

A nation, like a building structure, is built upon foundational supports. Verses two and three speak to the character issue, which is the first of eight supports that the prophet announces God will remove as a result of the nation trusting in man instead of Him. The first item in a list of character-related institutions, found in verses two and three, is the hero. What is the prophet announcing? I believe the answer is both simple and profound.

Heroes Are Men Who Are Selfless

Heroes do not create themselves. Throughout history, America has been graced with numerous examples of great heroism, but the fact remains, no true hero has ever created himself. That is not to say that some men have not embellished their own persona by manipulating public opinion. Even when a carefully plotted and skillfully executed strategy is engineered, if it is not rooted in fact, the truth sooner or later comes to light, and the hero is dethroned. O.J. Simpson is a recent example of a fallen contemporary sports hero.

What is a true hero? He or she is an individual, sovereignly placed in a given situation, where in a split second, when called upon, decide to act selflessly. Their consideration is someone else. That is why it must be a sovereign act. True heroism is always selfless. People who become heroes never plan it in advance. Heroes are ordinary people who, when called upon, do extraordinary things.

How does a man become a hero? In the final analysis, the only way to prepare for being a hero is to be faithful in keeping the commitments you make. The only assurance that a person will make the right decision in the "big" moment is by constantly rehearsing for that "big" moment through every seemingly insignificant small moment of life. That is what enables a man to throw his body on the hand grenade to save others from being destroyed. That is what enables a man or woman to refuse to run for "self-preservation" and rather charge into a barrage of bullets and fly directly into enemy aircraft fire.

Steve Farrar first acquainted me with Wilson L. Harrell. Harrell is a real hero. During World War II, while flying a P-38, providing air support to General Patton, he and three other pilots were ordered to take out a German airfield one hundred miles behind enemy lines. After the bombing run, he looked up in the sky and saw what turned out to be sixty-seven enemy fighters. They were a part of a crack group of pilots brought together by General Herman Goering toward the end of the war, and touted as an invincible unit.

Harrell relates calling to his leader, Jerry Gardner, and yelling, "Jerry, there's a whole mess of bogeys at 10 o'clock low!" In a moment Jerry replied, "Let's go get 'em."

What no one knew until the four American planes were in the midst of the sixty-seven German planes, was that they were loaded with bombs.

The Americans zoomed right into the middle of them. The Germans, fearful of hitting their own general, were hesitant to fire.

By day's end, the Americans had downed forty-seven yellow-nosed fighters while losing only one American plane. All four American pilots survived. Jerry Gardner, William Harrell and their two fellow pilots are genuine American heroes. Only God can make a hero. [60]

George Washington Was A Hero

How do you explain men and women who take such courageous actions in the face of seemingly overwhelming odds, not only surviving, but often not even being wounded? The answer is God's sovereign deliverance. We used to hold up heroes and their heroism to be emulated by our children. In today's culture, risking your own life for someone else is often derided as being foolish. The account of George Washington at the Battle of Monongahela was included in student textbooks in America until 1934:

> I am a chief and ruler over my tribes. My influence extends to the waters of the great lakes and to the far blue mountains.
>
> I have traveled a long and weary path that I might see the young warrior of the great battle. It was on the day when the white man's blood mixed with the streams of our forests that I first beheld this chief [Washington].
>
> I called to my young men and said, mark yon tall and daring warrior? He is not of the red-coat tribe - he hath an Indian's wisdom, and his warriors fight as we do - himself alone exposed.
>
> Quick, let your aim be certain, and he dies. Our rifles were leveled, rifles which, but for you, knew not how to miss - 'twas all in vain, a power mightier far than we, shielded you.
>
> Seeing you were under the special guardianship of the Great Spirit, we immediately ceased to fire at you. I am old and soon shall be gathered to the great council fire of my fathers in the land of shades, but ere I go, there is something bids me speak in the voice of prophecy:
>
> Listen! The Great Spirit protects that man [pointing at Washington], and guides his destinies - he will become the chief of nations, and a people yet unborn will hail him as the founder of a mighty empire. I am come to pay homage to the man who is the particular favorite of Heaven, and who can never die in battle.[61]

"Lifeboat" Clarifies The Wrong Values

A generation ago, our educators understood the value of teaching such life lessons to our young people. Now under the guise of "values clarification" our students are playing role games like "Lifeboat." The object of "Lifeboat" is to challenge students to clarify their own values regarding human worth. Careful not to inject their own values, instructors set up a make-believe scenario in which seven survivors of a sinking ship find themselves in a lifeboat designed to sustain life for only five. Students then must struggle with clarifying their own values as they decide who should be allowed to stay in the boat and who should be forced to leave.

The seven passengers are then carefully described, including their age, any health concerns, their professional training and experience, etc. Who would you discard if given the choice of a Nobel Lauriet winner or an aging drunk? What about choosing between an elderly man with emphysema and a healthy seven-year-old child?

Tragically, the presupposition of all such role-playing is that there is no God, hence no chance for a supernatural rescue. Today's secular humanists, dominated by a worldview that excludes God, assumes that in His absence we humans have not only the right, but the duty, to make life and death decisions based on the assumption that we must save ourselves for there is no other hope. This encourages a self-centered, self-seeking culture which places the highest value on self-preservation and the avoidance of self-sacrifice.

The Christian solution to "Lifeboat" would be to hold all life as sacred. All seven would then pray, from the depths of humility and dependence, to the God of Heaven for His miraculous intervention. Perhaps someone would then volunteer to willingly leave the raft in an heroic effort to swim for help. Ultimately, God would choose who lives and dies while His created beings seek Him for divine intervention.

The humanist, with his optimistic view of human nature, assumes that through rational and objective analysis, man would be able to discover who should live and who should die. In their worldview, the situation dictates the morality. If one must decide in a situation, between the worth of an old, sick man and a young, healthy child, it would not be immoral to sacrifice the old, sick man, the secular humanist would argue. A biblical worldview projects a more realistic view of human nature. In truth, a more likely scenario depicting human nature, would be the five remaining passengers then warring among themselves, especially in light of their not knowing when their rescue might come.

Would not it be better to have a little insurance? Surely four would have a better chance to survive than five. And surely three would have a better chance than four, and so on. Ultimately, without God, man digresses to the law of the jungle and to what Darwin called the survival of the fittest. Pascal is again proven correct: "Man without a creator either becomes a deity and goes mad, or becomes a beast."

The World War II generation produced many heroes. Some of them are still serving their country, like Senator Robert Dole, who gave up an arm, a kidney and two years of his life for our freedoms.

Today's Heroes Are A Different Breed

Today's heroes are more likely to be a movie star, a rock and roll performer, or even a professional athlete. True heroes sacrifice themselves for others. Modern heroes often indulge themselves with little or no thought for others.

I never shall forget my one experience at a rock and roll concert. I was preaching on a conference program in Houston, Texas. The night before I was to preach, Jerry Falwell was the keynote speaker. He began his message by telling of how he had just been witnessing to several teenagers as they were entering an adjacent auditorium to attend a rock and roll concert. I decided to check it out.

I slipped around to the auditorium where, as best I can remember, the rock group, "Molley Hatchet," was performing. I did not want to pay to get in, so I started witnessing to several teens outside. I struck up a conversation with one of the ticket takers whom I discovered was a Christian. He inquired, "Preacher, would you like to go in?" I responded, "Sure." As we entered, we discovered the group was taking a quick break. The auditorium reeked with the smell of marijuana and was filled with some of the saddest sights I had ever witnessed. Within moments, the lights began to dim and virtually every teenager in the building lit up a Bic lighter and held it in adoration as they chanted to their idols. Suddenly, the band reappeared and I witnessed what I would describe as a Satanic worship celebration. Without warning, my spirit became so troubled that I began weeping uncontrollably, as my shocked host led me back outside.

That was more than ten years ago and mild by the standard of many groups today. We have a consecrated layman in our church who builds sets and stages for such events. He has seen them all. The stories he relates will break your heart. As our culture has become increasingly hostile to Christianity, it has become correspondingly open to wickedness. The heroes of our young people, like Madonna, openly display their contempt for traditional Judeo-Christian values, opting instead for a life of immediate gratification epitomized by the phrase "if it feels good, do it." They become multimillionaires at the expense of our kids. The depth of the wickedness of the rock and roll industry will be explored in a later chapter.

In Isaiah's prophecy, there is a natural progression. Heroes are raised up by God. They, in turn, inspire the warriors to fight. The warriors, in turn, empower the captain of fifty and men of rank. Together, these soldiers provide peace and security for the nation against aggressors from outside the nation.

During Desert Storm, the United States Armed Forces performed with valor and precision. Patriotism ran as high as any time in my lifetime. President Bush, who successfully engineered broad international support against Sadaam Hussein and his Iraqi war machine, received incredible approval ratings among the American people. His reversal on his 1988 "no new taxes" pledge and the resulting stagnate economy, opened the door to his defeat in 1992.

Within days after the election, Bill Clinton, with his known disdain for the military, began an all-out assault on the U.S. Military establishment. Instead of viewing them as warriors, they were viewed as a social experiment. Our soldiers have been forced to lead the way in tolerance for liberal life-styles. Everything that the military has stood for over the past two hundred years is now being challenged. Restrictions on women in combat are being removed, and homosexuality is being tolerated. When General Colin Powell spoke out against the wisdom of allowing gays to serve in the military on the Harvard Campus before his retirement, faculty and students profaned him with the vilest language imaginable because he was not "politically correct." He was however, militarily correct. The morale of our military is being destroyed and valiant men with character and morals are abandoning their careers while increasingly our armed forces are becoming an international police force directed by the United Nations. This is in keeping with the Humanist Manifesto's commitment to a socialist one world federation.

A Word About Women In Combat

What about women in combat? Should a woman be allowed to do whatever she chooses if she is physically capable? My answer is: that depends on your larger objectives for the nation. When your view is only a matter of fairness to one person, isolated from the larger picture, a case for allowing women to serve in combat can be made. But let us broaden the discussion. As bad as the secular humanists want to deny that man is inherently sinful, the fact remains, he is. The purpose of the military is to protect American citizens from foreign aggressors. The only consideration that serious-minded military leadership (including the Commander-in-Chief) should be asking is how can we **best** accomplish our primary purpose. The answer to that question clearly eliminates women from combat. It also, I might add, eliminates homosexuals.

Let me explain why. Man has a sinful nature. Why do you think rape always accompanies war, even though every civilized national body has condemned such behavior for centuries? Why do so many good soldiers invariably contract venereal diseases while serving overseas? The answer is not hard. Their nature drives them toward behavior that God forbids. There are three ways of dealing with this reality.

The best way is through personal self-discipline. This is greatly aided through a genuine encounter with Jesus Christ and His life-changing power. "Therefore if anyone is in Christ, he is a new creation; the old has gone (the old sin nature with its evil desires) the new is come" (II Corinthians 5:17).

The second way is to restrain evil behavior by severe punishment. If a man knows that he will receive thirty days in solitary confinement for his actions, chances are he will restrain his behavior to avoid the punishment. In other words, he will discover he desires his freedom even more than he desires a brief but thrilling sexual encounter. (This same philosophical reasoning enabled me to restrain my desire to disobey my father after two or three encounters with his thirty-eight inch belt when I was young.).

The third method has become the method of choice in today's armed services. It is to deny such desires even exist, or if they do, to deny that they are wrong. Remember that one tenet of humanism is amorality. Humanism promotes the notion that there are no absolutes and that individuals are free to engage in any sexual activity they please as long as no harm is done to others. "...We affirm that moral values derive their source from human experience...individuals should be permitted to express their sexual proclivities and pursue their life-styles as they desire." [62]

Underneath the high-sounding debates on fairness and equal opportunity is the philosophical belief system that sees nothing wrong in allowing young women to bunk and live for months at a time in the field with young men. Even more tragic than that is they see no potential danger in gay men being placed in the general population of heterosexual men. This is an insult to God and a basic denial of human nature. It defies logic and common sense.

A Couple Of Scenarios

Let me describe a couple of scenarios to prove my point. Let us assume that all the barriers have been removed. Two hundred years of American history has just been discarded and finally gays and women can serve in any capacity for which they are physically qualified. Everyone agrees there will be an adjustment period, but we can live with that. We have made our decision and we are committed to it. All is well until the next war breaks out. Suddenly, a national draft is reinstated. What will this mean for married women with families? Suddenly, qualified women would be required by law to be extracted from their families, including small children and thrust into combat. The devastating effects upon families is incalculable.

Perhaps they would be excluded. (In our drive toward fairness and equal opportunity for all, this is debatable.) Fine, we will just send single women. How do you think they will fare, living for months at a time in a combat zone? Remember, we are debating national defense. Do we really want to add the potential emotional conflicts of sexual interaction, love triangles, sexual harassment and even rape, to the existing nightmares of war? Add to that the physical challenges of bodily functions. Are we ready to see men and women relieving themselves side by side in the field? What about the added physical challenges that a woman's menstrual cycle necessitates? If the issue for the military is being optimally prepared for war, there is no debate. Obviously, being prepared for war is a secondary issue for those driving this debate.

Homosexuals add yet another dimension to this debate. At least till this present hour, I know of no one who is publicly advocating that service men and women shower together. Men are too quickly stimulated sexually by what they see, illustrated by the booming market in pornographic photos of nude women. Women acknowledge this reality in their quest to look "sexy." Yet, many in today's culture, including our current Commander-in-Chief, are advocating this very environment for homosexuals. That's akin to turning the fox loose in the hen house.

Beyond that, imagine your own eighteen-year-old son, ten thousand miles away from home for the first time in his life, in a war for which he did not volunteer. He is lonely, frightened and homesick. Do you really want him confiding to a thirty year old, seasoned soldier who happens to be his tentmate, whom he discovers later is a homosexual? Is that a dimension that we want to add to a battlefield? There is no debate here if the purpose of the military is to develop the optimum defense strategy for our nation. It is time to stand up and say "Enough is Enough."

Gangs In The Military

The July 24, 1995, issue of *Newsweek* magazine reported a new phenomenon affecting our military that should concern us all. Several notorious Los Angeles street gangs such as the Crips, the Bloods, and Chicago's Folk Gangsters are now active in all four branches of the armed services and at more than fifty military bases around the United States. Gangs now stake out their "turf" on aircraft carriers at sea, and during the Gulf War, enlisted men were photographed flashing their gang signs.

"The military doesn't like to admit (its gang problem)," Sgt. Wes McBride of the Los Angeles Police Department, himself a former Marine, told the magazine, "because it destroys the image of discipline."

A street gang symposium held by the Justice Department in November, 1994, warned that "with arms, weapons proficiency and tactics, some street gangs now have the ability to effectively engage in terrorist activities within the United States," *Newsweek* reported.

Not only will God remove the support of the military, but also the very heart of the nation. Where does real courage flow from? Real courage and character flows from a sense of rightness.

For two hundred years, America's courts were known as just and fair, but today that is not so. Across America, we have lost our sense of rightness. It seems that often insanity prevails in court rulings. In America's courtroom, rightness is often sacrificed as lawyers increasingly see their role as being responsible for winning a favorable verdict for their clients rather than seeking truth. No trial in history has reflected this reality more vividly for the nation to view than the O.J. Simpson trial. Isaiah prophesied that God would take from Jerusalem and Judah the judges. Obviously judges existed, but in name only. Justice was lost.

Where Are The Prophets?

He also announced the removal of the prophet. Look around; where are the prophets in our land? Men speaking out against sin. Far too often, preachers are failing to confront sin. Today, in the church we are being told that we must be "seeker sensitive" and "market wise." We must be careful not to offend people or they will not return to our churches, or so we are told. Increasingly, pastors are allowing a secular mind-set to shape their ministry, rather than the Word of God.

While I have personally benefited from studying many of the writings flowing out of the church growth movement, I believe there is a dangerous temptation to become so "seeker sensitive" that we forget God. While we must remove every needless barrier that might hinder an unchurched person and make coming to church difficult for them, let us never forget that we gather for the purpose of glorifying God and lifting up Jesus. When we achieve that purpose, "he will gather all men unto himself" (John 12:32).

The most liberating verse in all the Bible for any pastor who desires to build a great church is found in Matthew 16:18 where Jesus said, "...on this rock I will build my church, and the gates of Hades will not overcome it." To realize that the church belongs to Jesus and that He, and only He, can build it, frees the pastor to preach the Word without fear or compromise. Pastors must once again see their prophetic role if this nation shall ever be restored.

A Word From Jeremiah

Jeremiah was hated by his government as well as his fellow preachers because he refused to preach what people wanted to hear. He wrote, "My people have committed two sins: They have forsaken me (God) the spring of living water and have dug their own cisterns, broken cisterns that cannot hold water" (Jeremiah 2:13).

As in Isaiah's prophecy, God forces the nation of Judah to recognize He has been faithful, but they have not. In spite of all His blessings, they have chosen to turn away. Jeremiah holds his own generation of prophets accountable. Chapter 23 of Jeremiah's prophecy was an indictment to the preachers of his era, and it equally speaks today. Read a brief portion:

> "This is what the Lord Almighty says: 'Do not listen to what the prophets are prophesying to you; they fill you with false hopes. They speak visions from their own minds, not from the mouth of the LORD. They keep saying to those who despise me, 'The LORD says: You will have peace.' And to all who follow the stubbornness of their hearts they say, 'No harm will come to you.' But which of them has stood in the council of the LORD to see or to hear his word? Who has listened and heard his word? See, the storm of the LORD will burst out in wrath, a whirlwind

swirling down on the heads of the wicked. The anger of the LORD will not turn back until he fully accomplishes the purposes of his heart. In days to come you will understand it clearly. I did not send these prophets, yet they have run with their message; I did not speak to them, yet they have prophesied. But if they had stood in my council, they would have proclaimed my words to my people and would have turned them from their evil ways and from their evil deeds."

Secular Psychologists Have Replaced The Prophet

Today, our nation no longer heeds the words of the preacher. We have our own television channels and radio stations where we preach to one another. Even within our own circles, most of the preaching that is aired would lead a visitor from a distant planet, who was unaware of the nation's plight, to believe that basically all is well. Today's preaching largely glosses over sin and accents the positive. After all, we are often reminded, people need to be encouraged.

We, as God's people, do need encouraging, however; preachers must also confront their listeners with truth. Proverbs 29:18 states: "Where there is no revelation (prophetic preaching), the people cast off restraint; but blessed is he who keeps the law." In Proverbs 28:13 we are told: "He who conceals his sins does not prosper, but whosoever confesses and renounces them finds mercy." Our nation desperately needs that message.

Who is preaching to America? Secular psychologists and psychiatrists, the "High Priests" of secular humanism are today's prophets. Many of them are committed atheists who deny that God or the Scripture have any value in today's culture other than the generally accepted words of wisdom offered by Jesus in His Sermon on the Mount and some of the wisdom authors, like James and Solomon. They advocate situational ethics and view mankind as basically good.

During the past thirty years, there has been a concerted effort to discredit men of God and the scripture, and promote the universal acceptance of the role of psychology in helping to improve mankind. We preachers have done little to help our cause with such notable scandals as the fall of Jimmy Swaggart and the PTL, Jim Bakker revelations. Much could be written on the hypocrisy of the press and how it treats the salacious behavior of men like Robert Lowe and Hugh Grant, but ultimately all men will stand before a Holy God and He will adjudicate proper judgment for all.

Christianity Under Attack

Clearly, there is a concerted attack on the clergy today. Perhaps it is the human desire to want to be liked that prohibits more pastors from taking unpopular, but biblical, stands against sin. Michael Medved, an honors graduate of Yale University and a host of "Sneak Previews," aired on PBS since 1985, has seen Hollywood from the inside. He produced a one-hour video documentary entitled "Hollywood vs. Religion" that exposed the shameless assault of the Hollywood elite on Christianity. In his 386 page book, *Hollywood vs. America*, he gives even greater detail.

He points out how the movie industry's portrayal of religion has changed during the past four decades. This is reflected in their portrayal of the clergy. During Hollywood's Golden Era, movie legends such as Bing Crosby, Pat O'Brien and Spencer Tracy won public adoration and even critical acclaim by playing caring and compassionate men of God. During the last fifteen years, virtually every character that has been a preacher or religious person, has been scheming, cunning and evil. In "Monsignor," released in 1982, Christopher Reeves, who played a priest, seduced a nun, conspired in her death and had dealings with the Mafia. [63] In "Agnes of God" (1985), the opening scene reveals a pregnant nun giving birth in a convent and then murdering and disposing of the baby by flushing it down the toilet. [64]

"Poltergeist II" (1986), featured a hymn-singing preacher from beyond the grave who leads a band of demonic, Bible-belters in trying to drag a family into Hell. [65]

"The Vision" (1987), featuring an impressive cast of major stars was a sci-fi fantasy about conspiring Christians using hypnotic TV technology to take over the world. [66]

"At Play in the Fields of the Lords" (1991) was about crazed and arrogant missionaries in the Amazon Rain Forest. Universal Pictures committed almost $30 million to attacking virtually every type of organized religion. In addition to portraying the Protestant missionaries as psychotic, repressed, obnoxious and mean-spirited, they also cast a Catholic priest as being filthy and cynical, while introducing a Jewish mercenary who is covered with tattoos and brags about his whore-mongering, all the while expressing contempt for his own Bar Mitzvah.[67]

Perhaps there is no greater illustration of the blatant assault on Christianity being conducted by the Hollywood elite than in the remake of the classic thriller "Cape Fear" (1991). The original release (1962) starred Gregory Peck and Robert Mitchum. Nick Nolte and Robert DeNiro starred in the remake. The subtle, but significant changes in the movie clearly illustrate how far the culture has shifted since the Supreme Court decision of 1962 to ban prayer in the public schools.

In 1962, the villain (Mitchum) terrorized the family of the prosecuting attorney (Peck) who put him in prison. In the 1991 version, the plot is the same with one major addition. Though none of the original source material even insinuated or alluded to such behavior, Martin Scorcese, the Director of the movie, decided to make DeNiro's character a religious fanatic. A giant tattoo of a cross covering every inch of DeNiro's muscular back informs the audience that this tongue-speaking, Pentecostal ex-con is a Christian. Throughout various depictions of unimaginable cruelty, DeNiro carries his Bible and quotes Scripture. During the climatic scene as he prepared to rape Jessica Lange, he shouts to her "Are you ready to be born again? After one hour with me, you will be talking in tongues." Between savage attacks on the husband, wife and daughter, he speaks in tongues. None of this appeared in the original movie. [68]

Where are the prophets? God has withdrawn this support from America. The pulpits of America are no longer aflame with righteousness. Those that are, are largely being ignored.

The significance of Isaiah's prophecy is chilling. God removes the external support of the military and the internal support of the prophet. Our founding fathers understood the importance of both. Our present leadership seems to understand neither. Perhaps that explains why Bill Clinton finds such affinity with the Hollywood elite.

Psychics, Spirit Guides And The New Age

In the vacuum of prophetic preaching, according to Isaiah, skilled craftsmanship is lost, and enchanters and soothsayers are found. I believe these references are alluding to the drift of our culture toward the occult. The explosion of the New Age Movement with its open advocacy of spirit world communications, has opened this nation and its citizens to an almost unrestrained invasion of demon spirits. Communicating with the spirit of the ancients is a biblical impossibility. The scripture teaches that a person's spirit either goes directly to be with Jesus, or directly to Hell, depending solely on whether that person is saved or lost. "Spirit-guides" which Shirley McLain and others so often advocate are nothing more than demon spirits with whom God unequivocally forbids any communication (Leviticus 19:31).

Today's secular culture accommodates psychics, allowing them to build their own television networks, as they promise to bring peace and direction to troubled hearts. When King Saul approached the witch of Endor, God ended his tumultuous reign. Though he committed many wicked deeds, including attempting to murder God's anointed man, David, on two occasions, it was for this deed that God took his life:

> "Saul died because he was unfaithful to the LORD; he did not keep the word of the LORD and even consulted a medium (spirit guide; psychic, etc.) for guidance, and did not inquire of the LORD. So the LORD put him to death and turned the kingdom over to David, son of Jesse" (I Chronicles 10:13-14).

Can a consistent and holy God do less to a nation that is increasingly turning to the occult?

> "See now, the Lord, the LORD Almighty, is about to take away...both supply and support...the hero and warrior, the judge and prophet, the soothsayer and elder, the captain of fifty and man of rank, the counselor, skilled craftsman and clever enchanter" (Isaiah 3:1-3).

"Those who manage the affairs of Government are by this means reminded that the law of God demands that they should be courageously true to the interests of the people, and that the Ruler of the Universe will require of them a strict account of their stewardship."

-Grover Clevelend
Twice elected President
of the United States

Chapter Ten

When Statesmen Are Rare, Politicians Are There

"I will make boys their officials; mere children will govern them" (Is. 3:4).

When I was young, I had a driving ambition. I wanted to be a politician. People typically react with astonishment when I tell them that. As you know, politicians are not held in high regard as a group, but understand, I was born in 1950, and in 1952 Dwight D. Eisenhower, a true American hero, fresh from leading our troops to victory in World War II, was elected President. Following President Eisenhower came John Fitzgerald Kennedy, America's version of Camelot. I still remember vividly November 22, 1963, the day J.F.K. was assassinated, and will carry the memory to my grave.

There have always been scoundrels in American politics, but up to and through John F. Kennedy, our leaders were revered, even by those who disagreed with them. Today, there is a growing cynicism in our nation that approaches hostility at times, toward all politicians. I would like to offer at least a partial explanation, one I believe you will discover to be reasonable.

Our history is rich with great leaders, who were in every sense, statesmen. The term statesman implies that they were men who placed the concerns of the state, even above their own. A statesman was a man of principle and conviction who was willing to suffer wrong before he would sacrifice principle.

Watergate And The Loss Of Integrity

In 1968, Lyndon B. Johnson decided not to seek a second term. Richard Nixon, who had served our country for eight years as Vice-President, under Eisenhower, was elected President. He won in a hotly contested election with Hubert Humphrey. In 1972, Nixon was on top of the world after his landslide victory over George McGovern. Then his presidency began unraveling as revelations of the "Watergate Break In" during the Democratic National Convention began unfolding. After months of lies, cover-ups and stonewalling, highlighted by the thirteen minutes of missing conversation "accidentally" erased from the Nixon tapes, Richard Milhous Nixon was forced to resign as President, on August 8, 1974.

To add insult to injury, it was also discovered during the same period that Nixon's running mate, Spiro Agnew, was also a criminal and was humiliatingly removed from office. Suddenly, for the first and only time in American history, America had an appointed President who was never elected in a national election. Gerald Ford, the Speaker of the House of Representatives and a Representative of the Fifth District of Michigan, became the most powerful leader in the world, though elected by a simple majority in one congressional district.

Throughout this same era, America was being rocked by social unrest. There were race riots in the streets as the National Guard was called out in city after city to restore order. Our campuses were becoming bloody battle fields as students protested the Vietnam War and spoke out against segregation. The '60s and early '70s became the era of dissent for America. Musicians became the prophets of the Protest Movement, and cynicism grew in America.

The Role Of Reporters

The growth of television during this era allowed the American people to see more and know more. Suddenly, reporters gained notoriety as they became TV personalities. In 1961, Dan Rather went from being a local weather forecaster on Channel 11, the CBS affiliate in Houston, to a national household name when he daringly chose to ride out Hurricane Carla, one of America's most powerful storms in history, on Galveston Island. After a lengthy electrical blackout during the height of this violent storm, Rather suddenly reappeared, launching his career. With time, television enabled many reporters to become bigger than the stories they covered. Today, many of the leading personalities in the broadcast media have become multimillionaire, able to market their services for enormous sums.

Instead of reporting the news, reporters often make the news by slanting their reporting to reflect their own world view and preconceived opinions. You've often heard the expression, "consider the source." Never was that expression more relevant than when considering where American's get their news. The vast majority of Americans formulate their opinions on everything from religion to politics based on what they see and hear on television and to a lesser degree, radio. Unfortunately, conservative, Bible-believing Christians are hard to find in the media. Thank God for men like Cal Thomas who offers a fresh perspective in the print media, but Christians who bring a "God is" biblical under-standing to the news, are all but nonexistent. The vast majority of TV news personalities are secular humanists, who are pro-abortion, pro-gay, anti-God and deny any moral absolutes. Very few of the media elite hold the values of most Americans.

Negative Campaigning

Ratings drive their industry and impact their financial future. Bad news always sells best, so reporters are always digging for the dirt. This appetite for negative reporting, coupled with the politicians burning desire to get reelected at all costs, is a breeding ground for divisive politics. It seems the road to election success now depends more on attacking your opponent and being able to tarnish his/her reputation than it does on your ability to offer viable solutions to society's ills. The low road has become the "go road."

Everyone loses in this negatively charged, opinionated environment as we shall see in chapter twelve. Instead of the cream rising to the top, it seems that often those with the lowest morals become our leaders. Campaigning has digressed from the classic debates of Lincoln and Douglas, to a continuous barrage of personal attacks and underhanded politics. Survival of the fittest once again best describes the process. In this era, "politician" fits much better than statesman. Instead of men who put the interest of the state (the people) above their own, we have men who give full attention to the polls - hence I like to think of them as "poll-attenders" instead of "politicians."

This makes Isaiah's prophecy all the more relevant. "I will make boys their officials; mere children will govern them" (Isaiah 3:4). What is the most basic difference between a child and a man, apart from the obvious physiological differences? The answer is their intellectual and psycho-logical differences. It takes years of life experience to develop your core values and to transfer learning to wisdom.

Children Shall Rule Over Them

Children lack the poise and confidence to stand alone. They need support, encouragement and even protection. Who has not witnessed a little boy look up in the stands for his dad after a called third strike? Laws that prohibit the exploitation of children reflect our culture's understanding of that reality, though in today's post-Christian modernism, many of those laws are being challenged. As our culture distances itself from our traditional values, statutory rape laws become harder to defend. They were erected because of common agreement that adults can exercise unreasonable influence on a child.

Nations, if they are to survive, require men of conviction and character in leadership. Otherwise, national interests will be subjected to self-interest or the interests of well funded lobbyists. When God withdraws His support, the nation finds itself being ruled by men who behave like children. Children often mimic other children. Children want to be accepted. Children perform only what is expected of them or demanded of them. Children can be easily manipulated by a promised reward. Children have a tendency to sulk or throw a fit when they are denied their way. Children can be cruel. Children lack discretion. Children act irresponsibly. The list goes on.

Any of the above characteristics seem to describe the behavior of our political leaders today. The Clinton Administration has spent more on polling the American people to discover what they want than any president in history, and many today are questioning his core values. This does not just apply to Bill Clinton. Unfortunately throughout our nation, at every level, children rule over us.

Even more relevant is the implication that a nation without God's support soon loses the value of its senior citizens. Ronald Reagan, the most popular president of this generation, was continually criticized because of his age. At seventy-two, many consider Robert Dole too old to lead our nation. America places enormous value upon youthfulness, and while it may appeal from a purely physical standpoint, the scripture teaches the importance of maturity. It takes years to acquire wisdom. "I will make boys their officials; mere children will govern them" (Isaiah 3:4).

"Let my neighbor once persuade himself that there is no God, and he will soon pick my pocket, and break not only my leg but my neck. If there be no God, there is no law, no future account; government then is ordinance of man only, and we cannot be subject to conscience sake."

-William Linn
Chaplain of the House of
Representatives in 1789

Chapter Eleven

Neighbor Oppressing Neighbor

"People will oppress each other, man against man, neighbor against neighbor" (Isaiah 3:5a).

As the philosophies of secular humanism have increasingly permeated our society, they have given birth to some unpredicted behaviors. A growing number of American citizens now dismiss the notion of original sin and fully believe in their own personal goodness. Though this may make them temporarily feel better about themselves, an unexpected by-product has been a growing spirit of self-centeredness. Nothing illustrates this more than a cursory review of the magazine covers at any newsstand. We have gone from popular magazines like *Look* and *Life*, to *People*, then *Us* and finally *Self*. American society is now populated with vast numbers of citizens who have lost all concern for others and instead focus on themselves and their personal "rights."

Neighborhoods Were Extended Families

Neighborhoods, a generation ago, were like extended families. In 1958, when our neighbor decided to divorce her husband, it was almost as devastating as a breakup in my own family. I remember standing inside our chain link fence as a child when he drove up to discover the moving van outside his home filled with his wife's personal effects and half of their furniture. A fistfight ensued between our neighbor and the innocent driver who was simply doing his job. The police arrived quickly, broke up the fight, and the van drove away. The neighborhood shared a sense of loss as they consummated their divorce.

Today's modern neighborhoods are closer to the medieval era of castles, surrounded by high walls and moats, with guards posted every ten paces. The United States, with less than 6% of the world's population, now boasts 66% of the world's lawyers. Los Angeles has more lawyers than all of France. Colorado Governor Richard Lamm says "Filing lawsuits has replaced baseball as our national pastime. 'See you in court' used to be a real threat. Now it's as common as 'have a nice day.' They help to feed America's growing appetite to 'get what's coming to me,' regardless of the consequences. Today, in America, you can get plenty." [69]

O.S. Guiness writes "Only in America could a man try to commit suicide by jumping in front of a train and then successfully sue the New York City Transit Authority for $650,000 for the injury suffered in his unsuccessful attempt on his own life. Another equally ludicrous lawsuit involved a fireman who sued the city for $5 million for the pain and suffering caused by a fleabite in the firehouse. In 1986, New York City was forced to employ 120 full-time personal injury specialists and to pay out $938.9 million to resolve claims, including $17 million for sidewalk falls alone. [70]

In America, decency and morality were the foundation for our neighborhoods for over two hundred years. When God became irrelevant and morality became situational, everything changed. A neighborhood ceases to be communal when people are afraid to leave their homes, live behind locked doors, erect high, solid wood fences and put iron bars on their windows for protection. In the '90s, increasingly everyone is viewing everyone else as suspect. If statistics reveal that a certain number of people behave a certain way, how can anyone be sure their next door neighbor is not "the one." The only way to survive in the "jungle" is to go on the offensive. Today, many citizens in America view themselves as victims and see nothing wrong with getting their part of the American pie. This appetite is fueled by unscrupulous lawyers, driven by greed, who advertise their services free of charge. "We don't get paid until we get you what you've got coming," they proclaim. "You did not start it, but we'll finish it," one such ad declares.

The result? "People oppress each other, man against man, neighbor against neighbor." The spirit of our society is becoming increasingly adversarial. Forty years ago it was generally understood that no one was perfect and everyone made occasional mistakes. Phrases like, "it's no disgrace to make a mistake" or "it's quite understandable that you forgot," or "don't worry about it" were heard often and truly meant something. Forgiveness was readily granted because the giver knew that very soon he himself would be in need of the same. Not so today.

People Are Lawsuit Crazy

Today, there are those among us who drive by a wreck and think, "Lucky dog, now they'll get rich." Our courts are jammed with lawsuits of every kind. Recently, in a widely celebrated lawsuit, a woman in New Mexico sued McDonalds Corporation for 2.2 million dollars and won. This amount was the equivalent of coffee sales, worldwide, in McDonalds Restaurants for a period of thirty days. The amount was later reduced, but the whole affair reflects the attitude that prevails among many who see nothing immoral with "getting theirs" at your expense. In this case, McDonalds Corporation was declared liable because when she drove away from the drive-through window, she spilled her coffee in her lap and was burned. Our nation is on a path toward self-destruction as citizens have become lawsuit crazy.

It seems our freedoms are destroying us. James Madison, our fourth President and the original author of the Bill of Rights, said in 1788:

> The belief in A God All Powerful Wise and Good, is so essential to the moral order of the World and to the happiness of man… On another occasion he wrote, We have staked the future…upon the capacity of each and all of us to government ourselves, to control ourselves, to sustain ourselves according to the Ten Commandments of God….[71]

Jesus capsulated all Ten Commandments into two: "Love the Lord your God with all your heart and with all your soul and with all your mind. This is the first and greatest commandment. And the second is like it: Love your neighbor as yourself. All the Law and the Prophets hang on these two commandments" (Matthew 22:37-40). The courts, the class-room, the newsmakers, the television and Hollywood industries have all worked in concert to either remove God from public discourse or to reduce Him as irrelevant. Tragically, they thought society could love their neighbors without loving God. We are now witnessing the proof that the death of God leads to the death of civility. Neighbors are oppressing neighbors. The older I get, the more I believe that the Creator knows more about how to orchestrate society than does the created.

"Republican government loses half its value, where the moral and social duties are negligibly practiced."

-Noah Webster, Statesman and Educator

Chapter Twelve

Don't Make Me The Leader Of The People!

"A man will seize one of his brothers at his father's home, and say, 'You have a cloak, you be our leader; take charge of this heap of ruins!' But in that day he will cry out, 'I have no remedy. I have no food or clothing in my house; do not make me the leader of the people.' Jerusalem staggers, Judah is falling; their words and deeds are against the LORD, defying his glorious presence" (Isaiah 3:6-7).

This judgment levied by our sovereign God and delivered through His prophet, Isaiah, is once again alarmingly relevant to America in the '90s. There are several strains of truth to gaze upon, all applicable to our society. Notice that an unnamed man, recognizing that the nation is in ruins, confronts his brother with the charge: "You be our leader."

In America, everyone acknowledges that we have major problems, but ironically, everyone is waiting for someone else to get involved. Few people seem to understand that America's problems are their problems. The genius of American government is it was designed to be...of the people, by the people and for the people. Everyone wants change, but no one wants to be the agent of change.

Notice also the response: First, the brother says, "I have no remedy" (v. 7a). He is saying, "I don't have a clue how to get us out of this mess." I confess that as I write this material, I am overwhelmed with the magnitude of the problems facing our nation. At times I have arisen from the table when I have been writing for hours and stared in a mirror, asking myself how I could be so arrogant as to think I could ever understand America's problems, let alone offer solutions. Countless men, far wiser than I, have refused to even try. Yet something inside compels me to continue.

When I was in high school I had a desire to save America. Watching the nightly news reports of our nation's unrest, I decided to do something. I was president of our Student Body and well-known in student circles. Steve Hotze was president of the Student Body at St. Thomas High School, a Catholic parochial school across town, which had an outstanding reputation in academics and sports. The two of us discussed our mutual desire to do something for America, so we organized a rally and parade through downtown Houston. Our purpose was to show the world that many students in America still loved God and their country. Texas Governor John Connally and a young black man named Alan Keyes, who was President of Boy's Nation, accepted our invitation to speak. Keyes is now running for the 1996 Republican nomination for president. It was a great success with hundreds of high school students participating, but America did not change.

I decided to obtain a law degree and enter politics. I was actively involved in student government throughout college. When God called me to preach, He did not remove my burden to see America change, however, He did enable me to understand what caused America to change in the first place. I became burdened to see America restored to her Christian heritage.

In 1974, I resigned my first pastorate in Maypearl, Texas, and entered full-time evangelism. As a twenty-four year old preacher, I was still determined to change America. I felt like if I could just speak in enough high schools, conduct enough pizza parties for students, schedule enough revivals and travel to enough cities, that eventually I could change America. After fourteen years of relentless travel, it finally occurred to me that nothing was changing except the ages of my children and my ability to endure the grinding schedule that evangelism demanded.

I decided that I would devote my life toward developing a great church in a major city, and perhaps I could change America that way. I was soon forced to accept the fact that it was not going to happen. Finally, after more than twenty years of ministry, I have come to the realization that no one will be able to change America. If America changes, it will only be because God intervenes. You and I must concentrate on standing for what is right and doing what we can. Unfortunately, most Christians are not even doing that much.

The second response of the brother when asked to lead, was to say, "I have no clothes" (v. 7b). In effect he was saying, "I cannot afford to get involved." In America, leadership comes with a very heavy price tag. Leadership has become so expensive that many good, godly and gifted men have said, "Not me."

First, there is the purely financial consideration. The expense of running a national campaign for office in America is staggering. It now costs as much as $60,000,000 to win a senate seat in California. When Ross Perot decided to run for the presidency in 1992, he announced he was prepared to spend as much as $100 million of his own money to secure the election. It now takes $200 million to run an effective presidential campaign. Formidable candidates now routinely dismiss the idea on purely financial grounds. William Bennett, the former Secretary of Education under Ronald Reagan and drug czar under George Bush has said repeatedly he would not run for president because the demands of raising such enormous sums of money and the inordinate expectations of special interest groups who make large donations.

Those are the financial costs, but there are even greater personal costs involved. In the modern era of negative campaigning and mudslinging, many good men are deciding it is not worth it. There is an old adage in East Texas: "A dog can whip a skunk, but it's not worth the price." Families can be destroyed in the course of a campaign. It is especially damaging to children who may have to defend outrageous lies to their classmates, or endure their scorn and derision. Heaven help the candidate who has a blemish from the past. The most admirable quality of Bill Clinton, exposed during the 1992 campaign, was his ability to ride out accusation after accusation attacking his personal character. Not many people are willing to endure such scrutiny and exposure.

Finally, the brother cried out, "do not make me the leader of the people." First he said, "I don't have a clue." Next he said, "I don't have clothes." Now he says, "I don't care."

Perhaps no attitude better describes the American political scene than those words: "I don't care." Apathy is destroying our great nation, and nothing more offends God. Throughout Scripture, the harshest language is used to express God's displeasure with apathy. In Revelation 3, to the Church of Laodicea, Christ says: "So because you are lukewarm - neither hot nor cold - I am about to spit you out of my mouth" (v. 16). To the servant who did nothing with his talent, his master said: "You wicked and lazy servant," and He had him thrown into darkness in chains" (Matthew 26:26).

When I consider the latent and untapped power that the Church possesses if God's people would once again rise up and become salt and light, I am overwhelmed. I would not be so foolish as to suggest that the political process is the key to revival, but I resolutely believe that Christians must be held accountable for abandoning the process. Someone is going to dictate the political agenda of this nation. I would rather see people with a biblical understanding of human nature and God's plans make those decisions than people who hate God and reject His Word. It is a known fact that the vast majority of evangelical Christians do not vote in local or national elections. The year 1994, was considered by many analysts as a giant conservative victory as Christians in record numbers registered and voted their convictions, yet, studies reveal that in 1994, only a small fraction of the evangelical Christians bothered to vote. What would happen to America if 75% of those who regularly attend a Bible-believing church turned out to the polls? The debates that rage in America over the right to kill preborn babies, dissect their bodies for fetal tissue research, gas our senior citizens, raise taxes by encouraging gambling, and legitimizing homosexuals would end.

When people refuse to get involved because they either do not have a clue how to approach the issues or do not have the clothes or they just do not care, it is time for revival. If people do not get involved, now, it is over for America as we know it. It is time for people to say "Enough is Enough."

"Can there be any doubt, hearing those echoes from culture, that a great civil war of values is being waged on the Western Nations, or that radical anti-family forces are making dramatic alterations in the way we think and act?"

- Dr. James Dobson
President of Focus on the Family

Chapter Thirteen

Offensive Speech and Illicit Behavior

"Jerusalem staggers, Judah is falling; their words and deeds are against the Lord" (Isaiah 3:8b).

In this, the seventh judgment upon the nation that forgets God, Isaiah describes a people literally staggering like a drunken man about to fall. How descriptive is his language and how accurate is the assessment when applied to America.

Both *The Humanist Manifesto* of 1933, and *The Humanist Manifesto II* of 1973, the updated version, dreamed of a day that seems to now be reality. Affirming that all ethics were situational and flowed from no absolute source, they effectively wiped away any reference points upon which society or culture could build acceptable norms for behavior.

"Ethics stem from human need and interest...a civilized society should be a tolerant one...individuals should be permitted to express their sexual proclivities and pursue their life-styles as they desire." [72]

The New Morality

The entertainment industry, more than any other segment of America society, reflects how the "new morality" has been embraced. "The Ten Commandments (have) in effect been replaced by Brecht's single commandment, 'be good to yourself.' " [73]

Aided by Supreme Court rulings, through which the justices have managed to extend First Amendment protection to obscene speech and pornography, today virtually anything goes. Irving Kristol writes of today's moral malaise, "I think we can all agree that the United States today is experiencing what we call a crisis in values." [74] Dante Germino, a professor at the University of Virginia, in agreeing with Kristol, writes, "...(a crisis in values) means that we have lost our bearings and balance, that we have become disoriented and confused, that there has been a breakdown of ethical standards, that we no longer know how to judge right from wrong." [75]

Today, anything is acceptable. The only wrong in the new morality, is to dare to say that what someone else is doing, is wrong. Truly, we are living in an era described by the psalmist who inquires: "When the foundations are being destroyed what shall the righteous do?" Columnist Pat Buchanan accurately assesses the war that is being raged: "The arts crowd...is engaged in a cultural struggle to root out the old America of family, faith and flag, and recreate society in a pagan image." [76] Dr. James Dobson, heard on over 2,000 stations, concluded:

> Nothing short of a great Civil War of Values rages today throughout North America. Two sides with vastly differing and incompatible world views are locked in a bitter conflict that permeates every level of society. Bloody battles are being fought on a thousand fronts both inside and outside of government. [77]

You decide if in America "their words and deeds are against the Lord." Michael Medved's revealing book *Hollywood vs. America* relates the following:

- In 1990, the National Endowment for the Arts (N.E.A.) contributed $70,000 of your money in the form of a federal grant to help fund a gallery show featuring Shawn Eichman's "Alchemy Cabinet" which included a jar filled with the bloody fetal remains from her own abortion. [78]

- Annie Sprinkle, who also receives funding from the N.E.A., is known for outspokenness on a variety of subjects. Her show features her masturbating on stage with various sex toys while she invites members of the audience to join her onstage where they are encouraged to explore her private parts with a flashlight. [79]

- In 1991, Ron Howard, better known by many as Opie of Andy

Griffith and Mayberry fame, helped produce a movie that won critical acclaim, if not wide viewership. Released by MCA/Universal conglomerate, the picture titled "Closetland" featured a male interrogator graphically torturing his female victim, whom he forced to drink his urine, ripped her toenails out with pliers, administered electric shocks to her genitals and penetrated her anus with a red hot poker as she screamed for mercy which never came. Apparently Opie has long since left Mayberry R.F.D. [80]

- On July 11, 1992, Time-Warner released the following statement: "It is vital that we stand by our commitment to the free expression of ideas for all our authors, journalists, recording artists, screenwriters, actors and directors." The backdrop for this high sounding statement was in defense of their decision to proceed with their decision to distribute the highly criticized song by rap star Ice-T, entitled, "Cop Killer." Lyrics included such advice as "bust some shots off"..."dust some cops off." Time-Warner said "(it) is not a matter of profits, it is a matter of principle...We believe this commitment is crucial to a democratic society...." [81]

- In 1991, Irish rock star Sinead O'Connor told *Spin* magazine, "I think organized religion is a crutch...Nobody has the right to tell anyone else what to think or believe...It's a huge abuse to teach children that God is not within themselves...That God is bigger than them,...That God is outside them. That's a lie.." [82]

- Madonna, in her, "Like a Prayer" video, falls to the ground in front of a carved image of a saint while worshipping in a church. In a frenzy of piety and eroticism, she simulates masturbation as she kisses the feet of the icon. She concludes by displaying wounds in her palms like those of Christ and seductively dances in front of three burning crosses. [83]

- The popular group, Guns 'n Roses, sold more than 12 million copies of their hit album "Appetite for Destruction" in 1987. Lyrics which practically every teenager in America knows by heart include words from the song "Anything Goes."

  "Panties around your knees,
  With your a_ _ in debris...
  Tied up, tilted down, up against the wall" [84]

- Their 1991 follow-up releases, "Use Your Illusion I" and "Use Your Illusion II" both dominated the charts. The hit song "Pretty Tied Up" described a young lady (not the term they used) who craved being tied up, whipped and abused by all of the band members.

  "She ain't satisfied without some pain.

  Friday night is going up inside her again" [85]

- Motley Crue in their popular song, "You're All I Need," take sado-masochism one step further:

  "Laid out cold, now we're both alone

  But killing you helped me keep you home." [86]

- The top selling album of 1991 was entitled "NIGGAS4LIFE" performed by a group of rap musicians known as N.W.A. - Niggers With Attitude. This album, sold to any 12 year old child with enough money, contained such songs as "She Swallowed It" which described a preacher's daughter who "did the whole crew" and will "even take a broomstick up the butt." There's more:

  "Because the dumb b_ _ _ _ licks out their a _ _ hole

  And if you got a gang of niggers the b _ _ _ _ will

  Let ya rape her." [87]

We Need Leaders With Moral Courage

I do not have the heart, nor the stomach, to print some of the lyrics I have read in preparation for this manuscript, but trust me, these are mild in comparison. These are the type lyrics that our courts can no longer decide are indecent. In the name of all that is decent and holy, if the men and women who lead our country do not have the moral foundation to understand the inherent evil contained in such lyrics nor the moral courage to say "Enough is Enough," and stop it, then I propose we systematically remove them all and find men and women who will.

In Texas, the farmers are known to say to anyone desiring to plant a crop: "Pray and grab a hoe." It is time to pray and take action if America is to survive. Do you need more evidence? Read on!

There Is More

- Christina Amphlett, the lead female singer of the Divinyls, sings on her hit album, "Lay Your Body Down...I am the mistress of the night, no stranger to your fantasy. Lashings of a recipe, I am whipping something up." [88]

- *Rolling Stone* magazine described her video hit "I Touched Myself," played repeatedly on M.T.V. for teenagers to enjoy, as "one of the catchiest songs ever on masturbation." [89]

- A girl group named Hole features lead singer, Courtney Love describing her experiences turning tricks as a teenager prostitute in the song "Pretty on the Inside." [90]

- Prince produced and sang "Sister" in 1980 featuring incest; "My sister never made love to anyone else but me. She's the reason for my sexuality." In 1991, he produced an album entitled "Gett Off" which vividly details twenty-three places to have an orgasm in and around your house." [91] In 1993, Prince dropped his name and demanded that he be referred to as 0(+>. His fans still refer to him as "Prince," "Minneapolic Genius" or "His Royal Badness."

Isaiah's prophecy again penetrates the darkness: "Jerusalem staggers, Judah is falling; their words and deeds are against the Lord."

Doubtless, some are offended by some of the preceding lines. Rest assured that I do not delight in either reading such perversion nor reporting such to you. I do so only now, exercising enormous restraint, only because it is past time for men of God to stand up and face the enemy. Our silence is not only damning the souls of those who are creating this filth without conscience, it is forfeiting our children and grandchildren the privilege of ever knowing the joy of the blessings that we enjoyed in this country just three decades ago. The lyrics I have quoted are mild. Many that I have seen and heard are simply unspeakable. "Enough is Enough!!!" Dear God, please give us time and grace to reclaim America for your glory. Amen.

"Even in purely nonreligious terms, homosexuality represents a misuse of the sexual faculty and, in the words of one educator, of "human construction" ...It deserves no encouragement, no glamorization, no rationalization, no fake status as a minority martyrdom..."

-Time Magazine, January 21, 1966

Chapter Fourteen

From The Closet To The Classroom

"The look on their faces testifies against them; they parade their sin like Sodom; they do not hide. Woe to them! They have brought disaster upon themselves" (Isaiah 3:9).

Isaiah the prophet now turns his attention to yet another character-istic of a people that forgets God and puts their trust in man. As darkness grows and the sun sets on a civilization, the vilest behaviors of human nature become acceptable. Again, I quote the *Human Manifesto II*:

In the area of sexuality, we believe that intolerant attitudes, often cultivated by orthodox religions and puritanical cultures, un-duly repress sexual conduct. We...do not wish to prohibit, by law or social sanction, sexual behavior between consenting adults. The many varieties of sexual exploration should not in them-selves be considered "evil"...individuals should be permitted to express their sexual proclivities and pursue their life-styles as they desire...moral education for children and adults is an important way of developing awareness and sexual maturity.[92]

The humanist's highest ideals have been realized in America. In the sixties on college campuses across America, students and professors called for the Sexual Revolution. In the '70s, streaking was the rage and hundreds of students across America took their clothes off and declared their freedom as all sexual taboos were discarded. The Woodstock generation knew no boundaries.

In the '80s, the sodomites, now called "Gays," marched out of their closets and on to Main Street to declare "We're queer and we're here." The revolution was complete. The walls of decency were destroyed and the age of amorality had arrived.

Isaiah's prophecy again pierces the hearts of Bible-believing Christians and speaks a relevant word. In the words of the King James Version, "The show of the countenance doth witness against them. They declare their sin as Sodom. They hide it not. Woe unto their souls, for they have rewarded evil unto themselves" (Isaiah 3:9).

The homosexual movement in America reveals how far down the road toward destruction America has traveled. As I begin this chapter of commentary. I feel compelled to share some personal thoughts.

Homosexuality Has A Face

Homosexuality has a face in America. Many Christians, as well as non-Christians, get quite emotional when this subject is discussed because all of us know one or more homosexuals personally. Many of us have relatives who are practicing homosexuals and it becomes difficult to face the truth when it is indicting to someone we love.

As I share the following facts and thoughts, please attempt to separate your feelings from the discussion and allow the facts to speak. Jesus said "Ye shall know the truth and the truth shall set you free." My intent is not to hurt anyone, but rather to speak the truth in love. Homosexuality is wrong. Silence in the face of it is also wrong.

During the past ten years, I have been called on to minister to a number of AIDS victims. Some have been just acquaintances, a few have been church members, a couple were personal friends, and one a family member. AIDS is a terrible disease that exacts a slow, painful death of its victims. As I have watched men die with this disease, it has become clear to me that whatever steps it takes to prevent the life-style that invites this dreaded killer must be taken. James tells us, "He that knoweth to do good and doeth it not, to him it is a sin."

Gays Demand And Gain Acceptance

Today, Gays are demanding acceptance, and since 1992, they are getting more than ever before. In March, 1995, Vice President Al Gore and his wife, Tipper, hosted a reception in their official Washington residence for gay and lesbian activists. To the activists, Vice President Gore stated:

> Its a wonderful thing to do what you are doing and that's devoting your life to others. This dedication is an outgrowth of the way you live your entire lives.

How is it that gay and lesbian activists live their lives? Perhaps he was speaking of such notable lesbian activists as his fellow coworker within the Bill Clinton leadership team, Roberta Achtenberg, whom President Clinton appointed to an undersecretary post in the Department of Housing and Urban Development, soon after coming to office. She is one of more than two dozen homosexuals appointed to high level positions in the Clinton administration, with hundreds more serving throughout the bureaucracy, according to the *Washington Blade*, a homosexual tabloid.

As a member of the San Francisco Board of Supervisors, Ms. Achtenberg helped lead a national campaign to economically damage the Boy Scouts of America on the grounds the leaders were antigay. As a result of the "wonderful things" she did to disparage the Boy Scouts, the United Way, Bank of America, Levi Straus and numerous other public and private organizations no longer contribute funds to a "bigoted" organization that encourages young boys to be: "trustworthy, loyal, helpful, friendly, courteous, kind, obedient, cheerful, thrifty, brave, clean and reverent."

Vice President Gore commended the gay and lesbian activists for "devoting your lives to others." As a good Southern Baptist boy, raised in the Bible belt, our Vice President is either (1) ignorant of gay lifestyles, (2) has narrowly defined "devoting your lives to others" to mean helping me get elected, or (3) he is willingly deceiving the American people.

Homosexuals Are Intolerant

Homosexuals who demand that their life-style be tolerated and even validated by all members of society, are themselves among the most intolerant of all. Ask the members of Pastor David Jones' small congregation in San Francisco. After printing in the church bulletin a small announcement that a guest speaker would address the subject of homosexuality, he suddenly found his church being the target of a hate campaign orchestrated by the gay community. A local homosexual tabloid displayed the event on the front page. Dozens of militant homosexuals showed up carrying signs and banners on the day of the meeting. For hours, they terrorized the congregates, defiled their buildings and chanted "we're here and we're queer" and "we want your children. Give us your children," in an alarming reminder of Sodom (See Genesis 19:5).

Though the police were summoned, they refused to help the worshipers and refused to call for more officers. The homosexual terrorists exposed themselves, simulated sex acts, and plastered vile and despicable posters throughout the building. They pelted the building with rocks and eggs. As they finally left, they shouted, "we'll be back, this war is not over. It has just begun." [93]

"Why not allow people to do their own thing? If someone wants to have sex with their own gender, so what? It's none of my business!" Is that a correct response? In the world of secular humanism, yes. In the world of Christianity, no. Why, because God expressly forbids such behavior. Why? Because He loves people He forbids all behavior that is destructive and dehumanizing. Is homosexual behavior destructive and dehumanizing? You be the judge.

What Do Homosexuals Actually Do?

Dr. Stanley Montieth, a medical doctor and author of *AIDS, The Unnecessary Disease*, describes what gays mean when they demand the "right" to their alternate life-style.

- 100% of all male gays engage in oral sex.

- 93% of all male gays engage in rectal sex. He points out that the rectum is not physiologically designed for this use and it results in physical tearing and damage.

- 92% of all male gays engage in "rimming:" the practice of licking the rim of the anus, ingesting various amounts of fecal matter.

- 47% of all male gays engage in "fisting:" the practice of inserting a fist into their partners rectum for sexual pleasure.

- 29% of all male gays engage in "golden showers:" the practice of lying on the floor, typically nude, and allowing a partner to urinate on them.

- 17% of all male gays engage in "scatting:" the practice of eating and handling feces. This often accompanies "mudrolling" or rolling in feces." [94]

What are the health consequences of this "alternate life-style?" Staggering as you might imagine. In the early years of the AIDS outbreak, it was dubbed GRIDS, which stood for Gay Related Immune Deficiency Syndrome. It was called such because it was almost exclusively found among gay men. Homosexuals demanded a name change and AIDS was a reasonable alternative.

While AIDS is the scourge of the homosexual community, it is not their only fear. While the median age of homosexual men dying with AIDS is thirty-nine, the median age of other homosexual men dying of all other causes is forty-two. The median age of death for lesbians is forty-five. That compares to seventy-five for heterosexual men and seventy-nine for heterosexual women. Only 1% of all homosexuals die of old age and only 3% ever live to age fifty-five. [95]

Is it less compassionate to warn a homosexual of the consequences of his sin and encourage repentance or to pat him on the back and tell him to continue in his alternate life-style?

Homosexual life-styles encourage a variety of diseases, among which are colonitis, mucosal ulcers in the rectum, and a psoriasis of the rectum and genitals known as Kobner's phenomenon.

Recently, a new epidemic has raced through the homosexual community. A group of rare bowel diseases, previously thought to be tropical, which has been dubbed, "Gay Bowel Syndrome." They include:

- Amebiasis, a colon disease caused by parasites. Symptoms include diarrhea, abscesses and ulcers.

- Giardiasis, a bowel disease caused by parasites. Symptoms include diarrhea and occasionally enteritis.

- Shigellosis, a bowel disease caused by bacteria. Symptoms include severe dysentery.

- Hepatitis A, a liver disease caused by a virus. This can be transmitted to others through food handling and through water splashing on toilet seats. [96]

Once again, science has validated Scripture. Predating scientific discoveries by hundreds of years, Isaiah warned Judah of the homosexual community's agenda and the homosexual's end: "They parade their sin like Sodom; they do not hide it." (Does that sound like a Gay Pride Parade to you?) "Woe to them! They have brought disaster upon themselves" (Isaiah 3:9).

Homosexuals can march on every state and national capital. They can demand and secure legal legitimacy. They can even force organized churches to license and ordain them or be closed down, but they cannot and will not escape the disaster that Scripture predicted in this verse over 2,500 years ago. Love compels those of us who understand the truth to warn them and to raise up a biblical standard for our sons and daughters. Love compels us to say, "Enough is Enough."

> "So thou, O son of man, I have set thee a watchman unto the house of Israel; therefore thou shalt hear the word at my mouth, and warn them from me. When I say unto the wicked, O wicked man, thou shalt surely die; if thou doest not speak to warn the wicked from his way, that wicked man shall die in his iniquity; but his blood will I require at thine hand. Nevertheless, if thou warn the wicked of his way to turn from it; if he do not turn from his way, he shall die in his iniquity; but thou hast delivered thy soul" (Ezekiel 33:7-9 KJV).

In our effort to avoid offending this generation, many pastors and preachers have lost the passion that drove Paul to endure beatings, imprisonment, stonings and shipwreck: "Knowing the terror of the Lord, we persuade men" (II Corinthians 5:11 KJV).

Not only are homosexuals literally killing themselves with many diseases unique to their life-style, they are contracting more conventional types of sexually transmitted diseases as well. Male homosexuals are fourteen times more likely to contract syphilis, eight times more likely to acquire Hepatitis A or B and hundreds of times more likely to have an oral venereal disease than their heterosexual counterparts. Female homosexuals are nineteen times more likely to contract genital warts, four times as likely to contract scabies and twelve times more likely to contract an oral infection than are heterosexual women.

How can this be? Inevitably it is an erudite, well-groomed, "together" kind of guy or gal that happens to be gay that addresses a high school or college campus to discuss the topic of homosexuality. They are typically lawyers, doctors, accountants, or some other type of professional. Their message is "all we want is to be treated like other members of society. We want to be able to own homes, adopt children, and express affection just like heterosexual couples do, without being condemned by society. We want the same rights as other minorities."

But the fact remains, they are not like other minorities. America has never before granted minority status based on life-style. Are we now ready to move down the path toward ascribing "minority status" and corresponding rights to smokers, alcoholics, divorcees, murderers, rapists, etc? Homosexuals and their supporters in academia and the print media love to trumpet every thread of purported evidence that seems to suggest that homosexuality is a biological phenomenon. Ironically, when the same theories are later disproved, or the results are exposed as fraudulent, or the means of obtaining data discredited, these same proponents of the homosexual life-style suddenly become deafeningly silent. Regardless of any "scientific" discoveries that may come, homosexuals will no more be exempted from the consequences of their sinful behavior, than Jim Bakker was with his illicit heterosexual encounter, nor anyone else who chooses to defy any of God's moral laws. God has not abdicated His throne nor dominion to man. His laws are rooted in His infinite wisdom and understanding of the nature of mankind, and are not subject to majority rule or the latest fad of America's social engineers. We do not have the authority to change His laws, and those who decide to ignore them and consequently break them soon discover a sobering and deadly fact: You do not break God's laws, but rather they will break you. Isaiah writes, "Woe to them! Disaster is upon them!"

Homosexuals want heterosexuals in America to believe they are just alike, with the exception of their appetite for same-sex relationships. Once again, the facts suggest otherwise. Gay men have between 20-100 different partners each year, and between 300-500 during their sexual lifetime. Sex and eroticism drives their culture whether it happens to be gay art, gay theater, or a gay bar. They engage in their sexual activities in public parks, roadside rest areas and malls where, in New York, according to John Paulk, an administrator with "Love in Action" and himself a former female impersonator, they have perfected the art of anonymous sex. In New York, he details, gays joke about... "Shopping Bag Day," the practice of one gay sitting on a toilet in a public restroom while another stands in a shopping bag facing him, giving the appearance of only one person being in the stall.

Bathhouses are the happening place for homosexuals. All but forced out of business in the eighties due to the AIDS epidemic, they are making a huge comeback today. Homosexuals can obtain a membership for a minimal fee. They then check their clothes as they enter, drape a towel around their bodies if they please, and mix. The central hall is surrounded with private rooms with either mats or bunks where orgies, not unlike ancient Rome, are endless. Multiple, anonymous partners are the attraction in the gay bath houses. An explosion of disease that threatens the entire nation is the result.

Men who love God, adhere to the Scripture, and cherish their families must wake up. Homosexuals, at best, represent only 2 or 3% of the American public. Though their sympathizers are growing, they still represent a small fraction of American citizens, yet they are capturing America. "How," you ask? Let me explain.

First, they are well-funded. Many of them are professionals with larger than average incomes. If they have a live-in lover, their household income is doubled. They have none of the expenses most Americans face for children, like college education, automobiles, or insurance, etc.

Secondly, they have time. Typically, they are not going to parent-teacher meetings, unless it is to advance their cause. They are not going to little league games, cheerleading practice, or church activities.

Thirdly, they have powerful sympathizers. Many of the educational and media elite have embraced the same amoral, atheistic philosophies that have given rise to the homosexual movement. Though they may not be engaging in the homosexual behavior, they detest anyone who forbids it on the grounds that it is wrong. They particularly detest religionists who do so on the basis of biblical convictions.

Fourth, they have the legal offensive. Many homosexuals themselves are attorneys and they are more willing to devote their time and energies to the struggle. The liberal bias of our courts for the last forty years, flowing out of the secular humanist worldview held by many of our nation's judges, has provided a receptive climate to the goals of the movement. The mere threat of the expense of litigation, not to mention the personal attacks often leveled by homosexuals against anyone who opposes them, has caused many cities and states to simply lie down without a fight.

Fifth, they play by different rules. In recent years, some gays have resorted to violence. ACTUP, a militant arm of the homosexual movement, does not hesitate to use violence to achieve their goals.

Finally, they have a plan. They have clearly defined goals and they know how to pursue them. The only thing standing in their way is biblical Christianity. What do they want? George Grant, in his excellent book *The Family Under Siege,* informs us that:

- They want to reorient America's whole view of sexuality issues. They not only want to end discrimination against aberrant behaviors, they want preferential and protected minority status afforded to those behaviors. In order to accomplish such lofty aims, they know that their number one priority right now has to be a full-scale development plan for AIDS funding and support. Utilizing the full weight of the federal government, they hope to accomplish at the national level what they have been unable to do at the local level: institutionalize homosexual concerns in the health care and policy-making apparatus.

- They advocate an emphasis on health care reform which offers them a prime opportunity to universalize coverage for behavior-related maladies as well as to integrate other homosexually-oriented actions into the medical mainstream.

- They are emphasizing the necessity to mandate sensitivity training in all schools at all levels to homosexual behaviors, life-styles, and concerns.

- They are pushing for an official implementation and prosecution of "hate crimes" as well as an unofficial stigmatization of "insensitive beliefs" or "hate groups" such as churches or private schools.

- They advocate that schools and workplaces help students or employees "overcome stereotypical fears" by exposing them to "alternative life-styles." [97]

I am amazed at how ignorant most Americans are when it comes to what the homosexuals truly want of our nation. If the American public could attend one gay rights parade down the streets of New York City, San Francisco or even on the steps of our nation's Capital in Washington, D.C., I am convinced the debate would be over. People, by the millions, would shout, "Enough is Enough!"

Isaiah's prophecy 2,500 years ago has become today's headlines when he writes, "Jerusalem staggers, Judah is falling; their words and deeds are against the Lord, defying his glorious presence."

It is commonplace during a gay march to see open and shameful acts of every variety in the streets with its flagrant, open nudity. As the marchers flaunt their deviancy to all traditional societal norms, they shout obscenities and lift up countless placards of blasphemy. Milder signs announce such things as "God is gay," "Jesus was illegitimate" and "Jesus was homosexual."

Their "in your face" flaunting of their sexuality is not unlike that described in the Genesis account of Sodom where:

> "All the men of every part of the city of Sodom - both young and old - surrounded the house. They called to Lot, where are the men who came to you tonight? Bring them to us so that we can have sex with them" (Genesis 19:4-5). Notice God's response to such flaunting behavior which He forbids: "The men of Sodom so provoked God with their aggressive demands, that He destroyed the whole region and every living thing in the region. Then the LORD rained down burning sulfur on Sodom and Gomorrah, from the LORD out of the heavens. Thus he overthrew those cities and the entire plain, including all those living in the cities - and also the vegetation in the land" (Genesis 19:24-25).

Isaiah makes an interesting observation about homosexuality; "The look on their faces testifies against them." Have you ever noticed most homosexuals have a certain look that is reflected in their eyes? The King James translation describes it as the "show of their countenance." There are a number of theories as to why that is so, but the fact is undeniable. As a rule, homosexuals cannot totally disguise themselves because it is reflected in their eyes. Jesus said:

> "The eye is the lamp of the body. If your eyes are good, your whole body will be full of light, but if your eyes are bad, your whole body will be full of darkness. If then the light within you is darkness, how great is that darkness. No one can serve two masters. Either he will hate the one and love the other, or he will be devoted to the one and despise the other" (Matthew 6:22-24).

This helps explain a number of things regarding homosexuals. Though they love to be portrayed as gentle, caring and sensitive human beings, do not be deceived. Many homosexuals can become very violent and appear to have no hesitancy to inflict property damage or even bodily harm to anyone who would dare to disagree with them. Scenes of the 1992 Republic National Convention in Houston quickly come to mind. Police officers in every major city in America can testify to the level of violence homosexuals can and will inflict.

When the truth of their life-style is graphically portrayed as I have attempted to do in this chapter, some will dismiss such behavior as unthinkable and choose rather to ignore it or disbelieve it. But remember the words of Jesus; "If your eyes are bad (if you refuse to receive the truth), your whole body will be full of darkness (your actions will become increasingly evil)."

When God created man, He made him in the image of God. Realizing that man needed companionship, God removed a rib from Adam's side and created for him a helpmate. When Adam saw Eve for the first time he was delighted and took her for his bride (Gen. 2:20-25).

The highest expression of Godlikeness that man can achieve on this earth is experienced when in perfect submission to God, a committed, caring, loving, married Christian couple express their mutual, selfless, devotion to each other in an intimate sexual encounter, where they are "united (and become) one flesh."

Out of that mutual and caring relationship they have the joy of taking part in God's ongoing creation work through the reproduction of offspring. The closer that couple gets to God, the higher and more rewarding will be their relationship, bringing both greater joy as God sheds His glory over them.

Enter Satan. As God is a God of love and light, Satan is correspondingly a god of hate and darkness. Satan creates nothing. He counterfeits everything. As a person rejects God and refuses His revelation, he moves toward the darkness:

"For since the creation of the world God's invisible qualities - His eternal power and divine nature - have been clearly seen, being understood from what has been made, so that men are without excuse. For although they knew God, they neither glorified him as God nor gave thanks to him, but their thinking became futile and their foolish hearts were darkened. Although they claimed to be wise, they became fools" (Romans 1:20-23).

Satan first convinces a person that there are no ill consequences to any behavior. Any difficulties that might occur are simply temporary setbacks that can be corrected, avoided or circumvented. Above all, Satan seeks to remove the "God factor."

As the eye is closed to truth, darkness soon moves in. The further into the life-style a person moves, the more degrading the behavior becomes. Instead of a highly exalted, mutually beneficial relationship, producing a "gift" from God, sex becomes a despicable and degrading act that provides a moment of selfish gratification at the expense of the partner.

Soon, it becomes a contest between two or more participants of self-exaltation, with progressively more sickening and disgusting acts. The further a homosexual moves from the light (God and His revelation), the greater is the darkness and the more ghastly and repulsive the behavior until the unthinkable is not only thinkable, it is done.

"Therefore God gave them over in the sinful desires of their hearts to sexual impurity for the degrading of their bodies with one another. They exchanged the truth of God for a lie, and worshiped and served created things rather than the Creator - who is forever praised. Amen. Because of this, God gave them over to shameful lusts. Even their women exchanged natural relations for unnatural ones. In the same way the men also abandoned natural relations with women and were inflamed with lust for one another. Men committed indecent acts with other men, and received in themselves the due penalty for their perversion. Furthermore, since they did not think it worthwhile to retain the knowledge of God, he gave them over to a depraved mind, to do what ought not to be done. They have become filled with every kind of wickedness, evil, greed and depravity. They are full of envy, murder, strife, deceit and malice. They are gossips, slanderers, God-haters, insolent, arrogant and boastful; they invent ways of doing evil; they disobey their parents; they are senseless, faithless, heartless, ruthless. Although they know God's righteous decree that those who do such things deserve death, they not only continue to do these very things but also approve of those who practice them" (Romans 1:24-32).

Foolish is the man who thinks that by ignoring this evil life-style that it will simply go away. The power behind the movement, as in the case of all the rest of the evils that Isaiah addresses, is Satan. He is not going to stop until he is forced to stop. In 1966, in the January 21 issue of *Time* magazine, an essay was carried that said:

> Even in purely nonreligious terms, homosexuality represents a misuse of the sexual faculty and, in the words of one...educator, of "human construction." It is a pathetic little second-rate substitute for reality, a pitiable flight from life. As such it deserves fairness, compassion, understanding, and, when possible, treatment. But it deserves no encouragement, no glamorization, no rationalization, no fake status as a minority martyrdom...[98]

Do you think *Time* magazine would print such an article today? Our culture has moved from a general understanding that such behavior is not to be tolerated in a decent society, to a growing movement to enable men to legally have sex with young boys. NAMBLA is now on the march. What is NAMBLA? North American Man/Boy Lover Association. Here's what NAMBLA has to say:

> NAMBLA takes the view that sex is good, and that homosexuality is good not only for adults, but for young people as well. We support all consensual sexual relationships regardless of age. As long as the relationship is mutually pleasurable and no one's rights are violated, sex should be no one else's business...
>
> Sexual liberation cannot be achieved without the liberation of children. This means many things. Children need to gain control over their lives, a control which they are denied on all sides. They need to break the yoke of 'protection' which alienates them from themselves, a 'protection' imposed upon them by adults - their family, the schools, the state, and prevailing sexual and social mores...
>
> There is no age at which a person becomes capable of consenting to sex. The age of sexual consent is just one of many ways in which adults impose their system of control of children. [99]

As I prepared to write this section, one thing struck me. Many otherwise excellent books addressing the moral decline of our nation, chose to either ignore this subject all together, or to give it only passing reference. I could not keep from wondering; why? Is it because publishers will not publish the material? Is it because of the fear of reprisal from the Gay community? After all, even the Scripture warns us that once darkness overtakes a person, they are filled with "murder, strife, deceit and malice."

Over the past few weeks, much of the laborious work of writing has produced joy in my heart as I have sensed God's pleasure and presence, but as I have read of the Gay life-style, watched videos of their marches and considered the Scriptures you have read, my spirit has groaned. At times, I have experienced fear as I have considered how some will respond to this information. Will my own congregation be able to handle such a candid discussion? In the end, my fear of standing before God someday and having to account for not speaking to such perversion overshadows my fear of man's reaction. My love for my son and my daughters compels me to take a stand against this wickedness that is covering our land and say, "Enough is Enough." Jesus said:

> "Do not be afraid of those who kill the body but cannot kill the soul. Rather, be afraid of the one who can destroy both soul and body in Hell" (Matthew 10:28).

Isaiah closes this section by saying "Woe to them! They have brought disaster upon themselves." Acquired Immune Deficiency Syndrome has the potential to destroy not only the homosexual community, but millions in the heterosexual community as well. I believe AIDS is nothing less than God's judgment upon this indecent act. I am amazed at how prevalent is the denial of such a claim both within the church and outside the church.

I make no claims to having all wisdom or to know all of God's purposes, but I do know the only effective way to escape the slow and certain death that AIDS brings to everyone who contracts the disease is choose to live life within the constraints that are outlined in Scripture. The only "safe" sex is "sacred" sex; sex conducted within the guidelines that Scripture defines.

"I love little children, and it is not a slight thing when they, who are fresh from God, love us."

-Charles Dickins, 1812-1870.
Renowned English author
and father of 10 children

Chapter Fifteen

Teenagers In Trouble

"The young will rise up against the old, the base against the honorable...youths oppress my people" (Isaiah 3:5b, 12a).

A walk across any junior high or high school campus in America today will convince you that America is in deep trouble. When Isaiah prophesied the conditions that would befall any nation that forgot God, he detailed America in frightening detail. Nowhere is this more evident than in the words "The young will rise up against the old, the base against the honorable...youths oppress my people" (Isaiah 3:5b, 12a).

Most inner city high school campuses are war zones, where learning has been subordinated to survival. Teachers and administrators are often subjected to threats and physical assault, while students increasingly turn to gangs in a desperate attempt to find security and safety.

Armed police officers roam the halls, aided by drug sniffing dogs and metal detectors. High school campuses have changed a lot since I graduated from Galena Park High School in 1968. Secular humanists have succeeded in their agenda to control the public educational establishment in America. They were aided by a coalition of liberal judges, the American Civil Liberties Union, weak school boards, apathetic citizens and a silent church. Remember, the lectures in the classroom in one generation, become the laws in the next.

The Classroom Was Secularized

I believe the following four Supreme Court decisions had a devastating effect upon the youth of America and the results are now coming back to haunt the nation.

- In 1962, prayer in the public school was declared unconstitutional *(Engel v. Vitale)*

- In 1963, Bible reading in the public school was declared un-constitutional *(School District of Abington Township v. Schempp)*

- In 1973, killing preborn children was declared to be a right, guaranteed by the Constitution *(Roe v. Wade)*

- In 1980, posting the Ten Commandments in a public school was declared unconstitutional *(Stone v. Gramm)*

In a span of eighteen years, two hundred years of American culture and commitment was declared illegal in America through three of these rulings, and our public schools became "gospel-free." Secular humanists proved to be great strategists. They recognized that the public high school was the one institution in American life where virtually every American citizen must pass, with the exception of a small segment who were able to afford private schools. They targeted public education as their center for indoctrination. The strategy was brilliant. If they could remove all vestige of Christian influence, they could then isolate young Americans for up to eight hours of philosophical instruction a day. They have succeeded. Consider our high schools today:

- Prayer is out; policemen are in,
- Bibles are out; values clarification is in,
- The Ten Commandments are out; rape, armed robbery, gang warfare, murder and cheating are in,
- Creation instruction is out; Evolution is in,
- Corporal punishment is out; disrespect and rebellion are in,
- Traditional values are out; unwed motherhood is in,
- Abstinence is out; condoms and abortion are in,
- Learning is out; social engineering is in,
- History is out; and revisionism is in.

A New Generation Of Criminals

Through the 1973 Supreme Court decision declaring abortion to be a woman's legal right, the children themselves were suddenly endangered, while the survivors were born into a nation whose conscience was being seared. We now have a generation of young people without a moral foundation, owing allegiance only to themselves, and committing increasingly more violent crimes. Law enforcement officials across the nation are alarmed by a new generation of criminals who show no remorse for their actions and no feelings for their victims. Life, even their own, has become increasingly valueless. Violent crime arrest rates among juveniles rose over two hundred percent from 1965 to 1990. Meanwhile, teenage suicide also rose over two hundred percent between 1960 and 1990. [100]

During the same period, spending on public education in America rose from 67.5 billion to 205.3 billion dollars in constant 1989 dollars. While spending rose more than two hundred percent, SAT scores dropped eighty points.[101]

Liberal secular humanists constantly insist that the problems faced in America can be corrected through education and environment. What they do not understand is the problem that our nation faces is a problem of the heart. The hearts of America's youth are being hardened.

Secular humanists have insisted since 1962 that God and the Bible have no place in American public education. They have insisted that evolution, an unproved theory, accurately satisfies man's deepest longings to know from whence he comes. Intellectual honesty and basic fairness should have dictated that children at least be given an alternate viewpoint that would allow for a Creator to be the initiator of all life. Tragically, our teenagers have been reduced to being nothing more than mere animals without a soul and without a Creator.

On January 21, 1973, killing unwanted children, as long as they were still in the developmental stages inside their mother's womb, became legal in America. By 1980, the seven-year-old survivors of the first year of legalized abortion, were protected by the Supreme Court from the dangers of seeing the Ten Commandments posted on a wall at school. No respected educator in American public education would dare imply to these students that they were created in the image of God. Evolution itself evolved until the theory became established fact.

The Survivors Of The Abortion Holocaust

Eleven years later, in the Fall of 1991, these youngsters were old enough to enter college. By 1994, panic was gripping university administrators and trustees across America because enrollments were decreasing. Finally, the effects of exterminating one-third of all the preborn babies in America began to produce measurable and predictable effects upon society. Perhaps the greatest effect of all has been on the psyche of these abortion survivors themselves.

In the sixties, the traditional nuclear family became expendable in America. No longer was it necessary to get married to have sex. Communal living became popular among the truly liberated. Old, worn-out, puritanical prohibitions were discarded and a new day of sexual freedom arrived. By the mid-eighties, no one dared to pronounce as wrong or unlawful your "right" to live with whomever you wanted, in whatever kind of relationship you decided. Many of today's teenagers have been forced to readily accept their parents' "right" to bring home a live-in lover if they choose. The traditional nuclear family was largely discarded.

In the Garden of Eden, God pronounced judgment on Adam and Eve for their willful act of rebellion to His command not to eat of the forbidden fruit. Man was consigned to work for his food by the sweat of his brow. Woman was consigned to bring children into the world through the traumatic ordeal of childbirth (See Genesis 3:16-19). God's judgment was swift and sure, but as always, the grace of God was demonstrated even in judgment.

While Adam would soon discover that his sin had affected the earth, making his labor toilsome, he would also discover a new principle in operation. He would find great fulfillment in the successful completion of a task. For example, at the end of months of labor in the fields would come the joy of a bountiful harvest.

In the same fashion, Eve soon discovered that though the pains of childbirth were almost unbearable, the joy of holding her new son made the memory of the pain quickly fade. Eve found great fulfillment in the bonding of love that grew with each movement within her womb during the development of her preborn child. The Scripture refers to that love between a mother and her child as a "natural affection."

Generation X

Today's young people have every right to hold a sense of betrayal and distrust toward the "Boomer" and "Buster" generations. Known as "Generation X," today's teenagers have witnessed the systematic extermination of one-third of their classmates. The two-thirds that managed to be born, arrived into a world where by age fifteen, 60% would be living in single-parent homes because the preceding generation invented "no-fault" divorce. The marriage contract has been reduced to be little more than "going steady."

After thirty years of being told that children would be better off if their unhappy parents just went their separate ways, we are now discovering that many children never recover completely from the emotional trauma of divorce. They often live their lives assuming the blame for dissolution of their families.

We should not be surprised that today's teenagers are resorting to so much antisocial behavior. Millions of their brothers and sisters have been slaughtered in the wombs of the very mothers that should have loved them and nurtured them. They themselves were born among a generation of adults too engaged in their own selfish pursuits to be there for them. Their fathers, in millions of cases, did not even bother to stick around to see them born.

Graduating from day-care centers where the vast majority are not the "cute" kid, or the "lovable" kid, or the "smart as a whip" kid, these love-starved children are often promoted to being old enough to come home to an empty house with their own key. No problem, Sally Jesse Raphael, Rikki Lake, or a host of other merchants of smut are more than happy to baby-sit them in their mother's absence. If those programs are not appealing, there's always MTV or VH1. They are more than happy to baby-sit the kids.

It Is A Matter Of Emotional Survival

They grow up cold, heartless and calloused, not because they want to, but because the alternative is too painful. My wife is a second grade school teacher in the Pearland Independent School District. We live in a great community, by today's standards. Her students are not inner-city kids, yet on more than one occasion, we have together, fought to hold back the tears, as she has shared with me the all too common stories of her children. Every year, she brings home a tale of pain that no child should bear, as a result of Mother's Day. In May of 1994, a seven-year-old child broke into heaving sobs when the class began making Mother's Day cards. He was forced to confess he had no idea how to locate his mother. My wife spent the day holding this precious child and encouraged the child to create the Mother's Day card in faith that soon he would see his mom and could give it to her. That evening, we prayed together for that precious child, that he would not be further disappointed. In time, apart from God's intervention, the heart of that child will grow cold. It is a matter of survival.

The explosion of gangs in our nation coincides with the death of the family. As Hollywood continues to choke America with its antifamily themes, the nation is being terrorized by teenage thugs. The most vulnerable of our society are our senior citizens. Unable to defend themselves, they have become easy prey. Isaiah prophesied , "The young will rise up against the old."

The Art Of Doctor-Assisted Suicide

A new American holocaust is just around the corner as today's teenagers enter the process of socialization and become the decision makers of the future. The abortion attack on their generation has meant fewer wage earners will be available to support the recipients of social security and medicare. Why should we expect them to make the sacrifices necessary to sustain an ever-increasingly aged population? The reward of self-sacrificial parenting is the security of knowing that your children will in turn sacrifice for you in your old age. Today, there are millions of parents who are unwilling to sacrifice their personal pleasure for the sake of their children as they grow old and infirm. They may well find those, who like themselves, survived the abortion holocaust and who were taught that they were nothing but animals that had evolved into upright carnivorous primates. The parents, without hesitancy, will choose to perfect Dr. Kevorkian's pioneering work in doctor-assisted suicides. I believe they will take his diabolical art to the next logical level. With their "Lifeboat," training, they are well prepared to start eliminating unwanted senior citizens. They will not have to worry about guilty consciences. Their training in situational ethics took care of that. Unthinkable you are perhaps thinking? "So was abortion when I was a teenager in 1960."

I am not attempting to justify what is taking place among our teenagers. My purpose is to put it into perspective. In the sixties, we ceased listening to God and started trusting in the godless philosophies of secular humanism. Isaiah predicted the results. Secular humanism, with its optimistic view of man and its refusal to acknowledge man's propensity to sin, has led America down a thirty-year path of destruction. Isaiah said it well, "...O my people, your guides lead you astray; they turn you from the path" (Isaiah 3:12b).

The August 10, 1992, issue of *Fortune* magazine featured an article entitled "Struggling To Save Our Kids." The entire issue was devoted to "Children In Crisis." Louis S. Richman, author of the article, pointed out that of the sixty-five million Americans under the age of eighteen, 20% live in poverty and 22% live in single-parent homes. Almost two million children under eighteen live with no parent at all.

Every single day, the author points out, three children are killed by an abusive parent and nearly ninety are removed from abusive parents' custody and placed in foster homes. There are now eleven million children dropped off daily at child care facilities and 1.3 million, ages five to fourteen years old, known as latchkey kids, are left without adult supervision, basically fending for themselves.

Richman also points out that over 500 children, ages ten to fourteen years of age, begin using illicit drugs every day and an additional 1,000 start drinking alcohol. The most sobering statistic he cites is the fact that nearly half of all middle school kids in America either abuse drugs or alcohol, engage in unprotected sex, or live in poverty. [102]

These statistics simply point out the level of hopeless despair that many teens call life. These same teens are taught in school and through the media that the environment is polluted, jobs are increasingly scarce, college tuition is prohibitive, the national debt, which they must pay, is approaching five trillion dollars and rising, and social security and medicare will be bankrupt by the year 2002. They have been abandoned by one or both parents, often sexually and physically abused, taught that there is no God and religion is irrelevant, and fed a steady diet of sex and violence through the Hollywood and television industry. How could we expect less than animallike behavior from them?

The Need For Belonging

Gang membership offers many teens their first opportunity to feel a sense of belonging. Unfortunately, illicit activity drives the gangs as they war over their "turf." The gang culture revolves around sex, drug abuse and power. Driven by their unmet need to be wanted and to be a part of a family, "Generation X" is susceptible to join gangs. To prove their worthiness to be in the group, prospective gang members are often required to commit a crime, up to and including murder. Drive-by shootings are as common place in American cities today as painting high school graffiti on the local water tower was thirty years ago. Gangs are increasingly getting involved in Mafia-style criminal activities. If you think that things are bad now, just wait ten more years.

Why should teens fear turning on adults? They have no fear of God and they have no fear of punishment. As crime has soared, punishment for crime has diminished. While we hear politicians continually espouse their promises of getting tough on crime, statistics suggest otherwise. The fact is, according to the National Center for Policy Analysis, when they factored in the probability of getting arrested, being prosecuted, getting convicted and going to prison, the median time served for each crime committed in America was only eight days in 1990. [103]

A Word About Punishment

One other important matter deserves discussion. No longer does our philosophy of incarceration reflect a commitment to punishment, but rather on rehabilitation. While this seems so commendable, the premise is faulty. Once again, the humanists' optimistic view of human nature and refusal to acknowledge man's basic sin nature, proves fatal. "Although they claimed to be wise, they became fools" (Romans 1:22). Rehabilitation presupposes that man was "habilitated" before he got offtrack. Whether because of the environment or lack of information through proper education, the humanist passionately believes he simply needs a boost along the way to get back on track. With this philosophy, any discussion of punishment becomes harsh, cruel and brutal. The ultimate penalty, the death sentence, becomes unthinkable.

Liberal secular humanists began transforming America's penal institutions in the sixties. Chain gangs, roadside work crews, and men working in fields along the roadways while guards toting shotguns on horseback became a thing of the past. New prisons soon began springing up with color televisions, state-of-the-art workout facilities, legal libraries complete with access to free legal assistance, college-certified instructors, free dental and medical provisions, improved menus and job training of every kind, all of course, in air-conditioned facilities. For the first time, the reasoning went, we will treat criminals as human beings and they'll return to society better people. Like a well-crafted football play, it looked good on paper. There is ample statistical proof available today to prove it is not working.

Unfortunately, for a growing segment of our society, prison provides better living conditions than the streets. Where else can a man get three square meals a day, free medical and dental assistance, and the opportunity to train both mentally and physically for a life of crime, in a warm, safe environment at the taxpayer's expense? Compared to living on the streets with its warlike living conditions complete with disease, drugs and murder, prison becomes the equivalent of R & R; a place to recover and relax, all the while preparing for the next time out. Add to that the additional status going to prison confers on a gang member, and the tragedy of this humanist lie is amplified.

The Bible offers the solution. Though it may not be politically correct, it works. Punish evil doers. That is right, punish them. It must be swift, it must be sure, and it must be significant. When the fear of the punishment exceeds the pleasure of the crime, then and only then is crime reduced. A child learns to obey a simple instruction when the fear of punishment is reinforced by swift application. Ironically, in children, the greatest opportunity for rehabilitation often follows punishment. When a caring parent administers punishment fairly and lovingly, the child's spirit becomes open to instruction. I have observed my own children, as they were growing up, commit an act of defiance and then wilt into complete compliance when confronted with the consequences of their behavior. Though it was difficult for me as a parent to spank them when their behavior merited it, the joy of seeing them respond so lovingly and willingly following the punishment, revealed the wisdom of God who instructs: "Spare the rod and spoil the child" (Proverbs 13:24). The same principle applies to every level of disobedience.

Solomon, whom the Bible refers to as the wisest man of his day, wrote, "When the sentence for a crime is not quickly carried out, the hearts of the people are filled with schemes to do wrong" (Ecclesiastes 8:11). "Enough is Enough!"

"The only sure and permanent foundation of virtue is religion. Let this important truth be engraved upon your heart."

-Abigail Adams,
wife of the 2nd President of the United States, John Adams and mother of the 6th President, John Quincy Adams

Chapter Sixteen

The Rise Of Feminism And
The Fall Of Fathers

"Women rule over them. O my people, your guides lead you astray; they turn you from the path" *(Isaiah 3:12).*

Bill Moyers, in his acclaimed television documentary, "The Vanishing Family," interviewed dozens of unwed mothers and teenage fathers in poor urban areas. Several girls related they could not afford to go to work because they would lose their welfare checks. A boy who had already fathered six offspring, when asked why he did not feel responsible to help support them, replied, "Ain't no woman gonna mess up my life."

Dr. James Q. Wilson and Richard J. Herrinstein have studied the current epidemic in America of crime, corruption and chaos. These Harvard professors have traced "the close connection between crime and the lack of proper moral training in the home. The failure of the family to provide a model of responsible behavior has filled our city streets with young people whose only role models are pimps and pushers, and our prisons are populated by kids who follow their heroes to jail." [104]

Defining The Family

During the Carter Administration, the White House sponsored a much-heralded conference on the family. Immediately, controversy erupted from militant groups who objected to the title "White House Conference on the Family." Their objection? The word "family" was too restrictive. The Carter Administration succumbed to the pressure and renamed the conference the "White House Conference on Families." This allowed them to be more inclusive. Now couples, whether heterosexual or homosexual, married or unmarried, as well as any type of live-in arrangement, including communal, could be included. Traditional families are becoming a thing of the past. So is our historic American culture.

The family is under attack on many fronts. Every one of the previous eight prophecies of Isaiah covered in the last eight chapters have impacted families, but perhaps none as dramatically as the feminist movement.

The Influence Of Television

I grew up watching a black-and-white television, as much as my mother and father would allow. Like children of today, I was fascinated by the images I saw on the screen. I became acquainted with each one and loved to pretend that I was "Sky King" or "Beaver" of "Leave it to Beaver" fame.

Hollywood made a contribution to the culture then, just as it makes a contribution to the culture today. In the fifties and sixties, "family values" were in. The Cleaver family featured a strong father (Ward), who knew who he was and where he was going in life. He both commanded and demanded respect from his children. His wife, June, was the epitome of womanhood. Their two sons clearly loved and respected their parents, as well as each other.

Countless other programs presented the same values, reinforcing the traditional family values upon which this nation was built. The "Nelsons," the "Harrietts," the "Cleavers," and a host of others, entertained and affirmed. As we watched them week after week, they reinforced the biblical model of a strong, wise, disciplined father who was committed to his family, assisted by an intelligent and caring wife. We laughed, we loved, and at times we wept as we lived with their families for thirty minutes each week.

Today, with rare exceptions, television depicts the home as a combat zone. The adult male figure is typically a self-centered, ignorant buffoon. The adult female character is typically strong, assertive and successful. The children often show complete disrespect for all adults and inevitably know more than their parents about every subject.

The Modern Feminist Movement

Betty Friedan authored *The Feminine Mystique* in 1963. Many point to the book as the spark that ignited the modern Feminist Movement.

In the introduction to the twentieth anniversary edition released in 1983, Friedan writes,

> I keep being surprised as the changes which the women's movement set in motion continue to play themselves out in our lives - the enormous and mundane, subtle and not so subtle, delightful, painful, immediate, far reaching, paradoxical, inexorable and probably, irreversible changes in women's lives, and men's.[105]

She then writes a lengthy list of examples of change, including everything from firewomen to women priests. Interestingly enough, she said nothing about the destruction of the nuclear family.

She did, however, mention abortion. "It is critical for feminists to understand the power of that choice to have children, and to keep fighting for the right to an abortion." [106]

Betty Friedan will someday answer to God for her role in convincing the women of America that being a mother and a housewife was not important. At least, unimportant in light of the potential that women possessed for moving beyond the home. She wrote:

> While I never found a woman who actually fitted that happy housewife image, I noticed something else about these able women who were leading their lives in the protective shade of the feminine mystique.[107]

She goes on to describe how some women manage to pursue challenging careers while doing the chores around the house, while others made the chores an all-day career in themselves.

What Friedan, nor most of her disciples, did not understand, was that the highest calling of womanhood is that of aiding her husband in socializing their children. Humanism, with its optimistic view of human nature, believes that all human beings are inherently good and therefore will respond positively to proper environment and education. Hence, all little Johnnie needs is a cheery day-care center, an abundance of activities and thorough education. This view believes that any adult will serve as well as a parent.

Children Need Parents

Scripture, on the other hand, recognizes that human nature is affected by sin. "For all have sinned" (Romans 3:23). "Surely I was sinful at birth, sinful from the time my mother conceived me" (Psalm 51:5). Knowing that a child's propensity is toward evil, and that a child will commit very selfish acts that can provoke a reaction, God designed each home with two parents. First, a father who would connote authority and demand obedience. The father's role would be that of an instructor and an enforcer. Fathers are commanded in Scripture to, "...not exasperate your children; instead bring them up in the training and instruction of the Lord." Children are reminded in the Proverbs that a father disciplines the son he loves (Proverbs 3:11-12). Why? Because the father understands that if the son is left to himself, without adult supervision and guidance, he will never conquer the inner urges to rebel. Proverbs again reminds us: "Like a city whose walls are broken down is a man who lacks self control" (Proverbs 25:28).

No child wants to share a toy. No child wants to pick up the toys when he is finished. The selfish sin nature within does not want to obey the simplest command. Who has not witnessed a beautiful, loving child throw a temper tantrum, simply because he did not get his way? If that behavior is not conscientiously and faithfully corrected with punishment when necessary, that child will be destroyed. The same evil nature will erupt when a teacher says "sit down," or a coach says "line up," or an employer says "sweep it again," or a policeman says "halt."

The home, designed by God, in the Scripture, included a kind, loving and encouraging mother serving alongside the father. It has often been observed that as the father is the "head" of the home, the mom is the "heart" of the home. During those difficult nine months of carrying the child, a special bond takes place between mother and child. As she unselfishly accommodates that small, dependent, trusting baby within by changing her life-style, her eating habits and even sacrificing her own body, the miracle of motherhood transpires. Perhaps that is why mothers always seem to have more tolerance, more forbearance and more patience with a child than their fathers typically show. A mother, more so than a baby-sitter or nanny, will endure endless nights of tending to a sick child, washing clothes, changing diapers, endless feedings, etc. Mother can be firm, but loving, when little Johnnie throws his temper tantrums. Often, only mother's shoulder will do when Johnnie simply wants to be held. All of this, and more, is essential in nurturing a child, so that the child becomes a genuine contributor to society.

In Isaiah's prophecy on the nation that forgets God, something interesting unfolds that is easily missed. Like a drunken man, first staggering and then falling, so is the nation that begins trusting in man. Verses eight and nine describe an attack on manhood until the ultimate perversion of manhood takes place; homosexuality.

Verses 12a and 5b describe an attack on childhood until the ultimate perversion takes place; youth rebellion. Verse 12b describes an attack on womanhood until the ultimate perversion of womanhood takes place; insubordination. When read in its entirety, Isaiah is describing an attack on the family.

No nation can long survive without strong, loving and caring nuclear families. God designed the family to be a place of growth, protection, affirmation, strength, and nurturing, headed by a strong father and a supportive mother. Together, they were assigned the privilege of sharing in the ongoing creation miracle, as their love relationship produced the next generation.

The Blessing Of Family

It has been my joy to be married to the former Tommye Glyn Adams, of Nacogdoches, Texas, since December 27, 1970. We have enjoyed a wonderful and loving relationship through the years. She is still the most beautiful woman I have ever known. She is not only my wife, she is also my friend.

On August 14, 1974, Misty Dawn arrived one month and one day overdue and weighing 9 pounds and 6 ounces. She has been a joy to our home. January 14, 1977, the boy I had expected when Misty arrived, was born. Richard Wayne, Jr. surpassed even my highest expectations and continues to be a complete blessing to his father. On May 9, 1979, proving that the best efforts of birth control can sometimes fail, Kathryn Ann arrived. We lovingly refer to her as our missionary, because though we did not plan for her, she has truly been a blessing from God. Our life would be incomplete without our children.

Misty was married on May 7, 1994. She and my son-in-law, Daniel Allmond, are now serving their Lord with devotion and dedication. Richard is attending college. Kathryn graduates from high school in May of 1997.

Over the past twenty-five years, our family has faced some difficult assignments, many which are too personal to share in the pages of this book. We have also shared in some incredible victories. It is not easy being a family, but I have now been married long enough to say with authority that God had our best in mind when He instructed man to take one woman for life. There is nothing in this life that approaches the joy and sense of wholeness that comes as a result of a lifelong family relationship.

I love each one of my three children with all my heart...and they know I do. I also know they love me unconditionally. They have no fear of the present because they know I am here for them. I have no fear of the future because I know they will be there for me. In Tommye, I have a wife, an encourager, a prayer supporter and best of all, a friend. I am all of that to her as well. We are a family.

The Lie Of Feminism

Feminism has lied to the American woman. Rooted in self, as is all of humanism, feminism has propagated a lie that says real fulfillment for a woman does not come until all the shackles of subjugation are removed. That includes marriage, children and sexual inhibition. In an effort to compete with men, feminism has robbed women in this country of the privilege of being women. The result has been the dissolution of the family and the loss of personal identity for many women.

According to feminism, at no point have men more dominated women than in terms of sexual expression. Pregnancy was declared the ultimate abdication of personal rights. Hence, legalized abortion in America became absolutely essential if women would ever be free of male dominance.

In 1973, in *Roe v. Wade*, the Supreme Court overruled the laws of every sovereign state and declared the mother's womb to be the most dangerous place to be in America. Since that day, the American holocaust now exceeds 40 million and is climbing by the alarming rate of 1.5 million abortions a year.

The Truth About Abortion

In 1979, C. Everett Koop, the former Surgeon General of the United States, and Francis A. Schaeffer, coauthored *Whatever Happened To The Human Race*. They wrote:

> Of all the subjects relating to the erosion of the sanctity of human life, abortion is the keystone. It is the first and crucial issue that has been overwhelming in changing attitudes toward the value of life in general. [108]

Of the *Roe v. Wade* decision of the Supreme Court, Dr. John T. Noonan, professor of law at the University of California at Berkeley, said:

By virtue of its opinions, human life has less protection in the United States today than at any time since the inception of this country. By virtue of its opinions, human life has less protection in the United States than any country in the Western World. [109]

Until America drifted away from God, slaughtering unborn children was unthinkable. Today, it is not only thinkable; to millions of Americans, denying a woman access to an abortion is now unthinkable. One third of the babies conceived in America are now aborted each year. I read the story of Ms. Sam Griggs some time ago in a publication. It graphically illustrates the tragic story of many. Sam graduated from nursing school in 1979, and went to work for a doctor specializing in obstetrics. It did not take her long to realize that his office was primarily an abortion clinic rather than a place for pregnant women to receive prenatal care, as she had been led to believe.

During her second week there, she prepared a seventeen year old for her third abortion. When she asked her why she did not use birth control, the young lady informed her that abortion was her birth control. She said she did not like other methods. Abortion was convenient and it was free. Medicaid paid for every cent. Sam soon realized that the public health center was referring a great number of girls to their clinic. Workers at the clinic were directed by officials at the public health center not to counsel the girls or even ask them about birth control.

Created By The Creator

Sam tells horrifying stories of her experience in an abortion clinic. Like the life-style of homosexuals, most Americans have no comprehension of how depraved are the proceedings behind closed doors in abortuaries across America. The founding fathers certainly had no misconceptions about the importance of life and the government's role in protecting it.

The opening lines of the Declaration of Independence reads:

We hold these truths to be self evident, that all men are created equal; that they are endowed by their Creator with certain unalienable rights; that among these, are life, liberty, and the pursuit of happiness.

The sovereign hand of God in the writing of these lines is reflected in their choice of words "created by their Creator." Long before the debate over a woman's right to choose an abortion, our founding fathers affirmed their Christian worldview by referring to the fact that a Supreme Being created mankind and in so doing, He endowed mankind with the right to live. That right presupposes the right to be born.

Abortion is murder. Proverbs 6:17 states that God hates, "...hands that shed innocent blood." There is now the blood of over 35 million children dripping from the hands of doctors, nurses and their assistants who continue in their brutal profession to this present moment. Not only has America authorized this slaughter, but now it has a president that promotes it: this is an affront to our Holy God.

President Bill Clinton signed an executive order on his third day in office lifting the ban on fetal tissue research. In abortuaries across America today, teams of doctors and their assistants now routinely abort full-term, preborn children in their mother's birth canal. These are children who are perfectly capable of sustaining life. They then insert a needle into their cranium and extract their brain cells. While the infant is writhing in pain, doctors then begin the dastardly business of retrieving usable organs for future marketing. Body parts are a lucrative financial by-product of abortion.

Three Techniques For Abortion

There are three commonly used techniques for abortion. The technique used often to end early pregnancies is called "dilation and curettage" or "D and C." This procedure is typically carried out during the first fourteen weeks of pregnancy. Entering through the mother's vagina, the cervix is stretched to permit the insertion of a tiny instrument similar to a small hoe, called a curette. The surgeon then scrapes the uterus. As he does so, he cuts the preborn body, created by God in His own image (see Psalm 139:13-15), into small pieces. He continues until the placenta is completely scraped from the uterine wall. There is considerable bleeding involved in this procedure.

During the first trimester, or first thirteen weeks, there is an alternate procedure used quite frequently, called the "suction" method. A power-ful suction is applied as a tube is inserted through the dilated cervix into the uterus. The suction is so strong it literally rips to shreds the developing child, sucking the baby and placenta from the mother's womb, pieces at a time, into a jar. The smaller parts of the body are still recognizable in the jars. This is the abortion procedure of choice by many abortionists.

When there is a fear of excessive bleeding in the expectant mother, abortionists often employ what is called a "saline" abortion or "salting out." This procedure is usually chosen when the preborn child is beyond sixteen weeks of development.

A saline abortion is performed by inserting a long needle through the mother's abdomen directly into the sac. The abortionist then injects a solution of concentrated salt into the amniotic fluid in the sac surrounding the baby. The outer layer of the skin of the little child is burned off by the high concentration of salt. It takes about an hour for the baby to die. Nothing that was ever done in a Nazi concentration camp exceeds this act in horror. As the father of three precious children, I weep as I write these lines. How can the Church of the living God be silent while millions of babies are being systematically tortured and destroyed, not to mention the lingering effects on innocent young mothers who are denied the privilege of even knowing what they are doing until it is too late? Usually about a day later, the mother goes into labor and delivers a dead, shriveled baby. Is this not "Enough?"

The Personal Cost Of Abortion

We have a precious Christian lady in our church. She and her husband are passionately committed to pro-life, antiabortion activism. Before she met the life-changing, emotion-healing, forgiving God through His Son, Jesus Christ, she went through an abortion. While the provider of the abortion made hundreds of dollars in an afternoon, she left with an emotional scar she will bear until she dies. Like teenagers who harden their hearts in an effort to survive, America is slowly witnessing the emotional death of millions of women as they buy into the wicked, secular humanist lie of feminism.

Nothing is more embarrassing to an abortionist than for a baby to survive a salt solution. This is far more common than the abortionists want the American public to know. As early in the holocaust as January, 1977, Dr. William G. Wadill, Jr., an obstetrician in California, was indicted and tried for allegedly strangling to death a baby born alive following a saline abortion. Survivors of attempted saline abortions are now living in America, speaking out against this brutality that the feminist and their accomplices proclaim is their "right."

It is significant to note who stands on the side of the "right to kill babies" in the abortion debate. During the 1992 Republican National Convention held in Houston, Texas, hundreds of Christians, joined by non-Christians who believed life to be sacred, stood on one side of the street. They were picketing the Planned Parenthood Clinic that Judge Eileen O'Neil declared to be off-limits to pro-life protesters. Most were singing songs like "Jesus Loves The Little Children" and praying. Across the street were hundreds of other Americans. They were militant gays, some in "drag," feminists, atheists and humanists. Some shouted curses at us and openly blasphemed God. Their contempt for Christianity was clear.

Between the two opposing sides were dozens of Houston police officers, wearing bullet-proof vests and prepared for a potential riot. One of the officers told my companion, "We're here to protect the Christians. If we left, some of these people are capable of killing you." There is so much more that I could say on this subject, but how much needs to be said?

When are Christian men going to realize what is happening in America and stand up to be counted? Today, these emissaries of death are conducting abortions on full-term babies. Do you know what the difference is between a baby at fullterm, but still in the womb, and a baby that is allowed to be born? About 15 minutes. That is all, yet it is legal to kill the unborn baby at full term.

Listen to the words of Isaiah:

"O my people, your guides lead you astray." In the preceding chapter he exhorts us to "Come, let us go up to the mountain of the LORD, to the house of the God of Jacob. He will teach us his ways, so that we may walk in his paths" (Isaiah 2:3).

Tragically, as a nation, we have chosen to put our trust in man. Now man is leading our nation astray. Isaiah even eludes to the latest trend in American education; revisionist history, when he writes, "they turn you from the path."

Those who are anti-God and anti-Christian in America have infiltrated the highest levels of the educational establishment. They have a philosophical commitment to eliminating any vestige of biblical Christianity from American thought and life. They are well-positioned, well-funded and well-connected. They are a very small minority in America, yet their level of commitment is rarely matched among Christians.

If these people were intellectually honest, Christians would have no difficulty repudiating their arguments for removing God from the classroom. All that would be necessary would be a study of history. Christians are losing the war of ideas because many fail to understand the nature of the enemy. Many within the church are so busy trying to prove they are kind, loving and gentle, that they have allowed secular humanists to steal the national soul. Instead of winning over our enemies, we have lost our culture.

Not confronting the abomination of sodomy in an effort to be loving to the sodomite, is not true love at all. It is the highest expression of self-love, which is sin. While the homosexual no longer feels guilt because laws have been changed and many within the church have been silent, homosexuals are now dying by the millions with torturous diseases.

Not confronting the abomination of abortion in an effort to be loving to the murderers and their accomplices, is not true love at all. It is the highest expression of self-love, which is sin. While the abortionists and women who patronize them may no longer feel guilt because laws have been changed, and many within the church have been silent, babies continue to be butchered, mothers continue to be emotionally damaged, and the healing profession continues to be tainted by innocent blood.

Now the same spirit of death and deceit is invading the educational establishment. American history is routinely ignored or rewritten to accommodate the humanist, atheistic world view. The role of Christianity is being systematically denied or ignored in today's classroom. Christians must remember while there is still enough residue of Judeo-Christian influence in our nation, that people who will embrace homosexual behavior as acceptable and normal and who will allow and even advocate the slaughter of innocent babies, have no difficulty, whatever, in lying about history. As they rewrite our history, they are not only leading people astray, they are destroying the pathway back to the truth. Selfless love demands that we stand up for the truth. If we refuse, America is lost. Selfless love demands that we stand up and shout: "Enough is Enough!"

"O my people, your guides lead you astray; they turn you from the path" (Isaiah 3:12).

SECTION THREE

The Hedge Is Restored As The American Dream Is Reborn

Introduction

Six days before Christmas, 1993, I received one of those phone calls that every pastor in America is all too accustomed to receiving. I learned through one of our faithful Bible study leaders that a family who had been visiting our church had been victimized by four armed gunmen and that one of the members of the family had been shot.

My wife and I headed for Ben Taub Hospital in downtown Houston. On the way, I used my cellular phone to gather more details. One of the intruders, I discovered, had entered a home and apparently shot the lady of the house. I met the Bible study teacher who had earlier called, at the hospital with the lady's husband. We stayed with him and offered what comfort we could as the bits and pieces of the story unfolded.

The family that was attacked represents what America is really all about. He is a very successful businessman, coordinating multimillion dollar construction projects all over America as a vice president with his company, in charge of construction. He, his wife, and their three beautiful children lived in a beautiful home just south of Houston in the western edge of Pearland, in a picturesque community built around a golf course.

On that fateful evening, they were casually enjoying their home. After attending church earlier that day, as they did every Sunday, their oldest son and a close friend were playing basketball in the driveway. The rest of the family was enjoying a television program in the family room. Underneath their brightly lit Christmas tree were stacks of wrapped presents.

Suddenly, as if out of nowhere, four men, three of them wearing masks, appeared in their midst. The one who was not wearing a mask was carrying a shotgun. In the moments that followed, the victims, like thousands of other solid, American citizens every day, saw their American dream turned into an American nightmare.

The victims were ordered to lie on the floor in the family room, while the four men ransacked the house. Their family dog, Chelsea, was predictably nervous and upset. The mother was attempting to comfort her youngest child, as well as calm down Chelsea, fearful he might anger one of the intruders. The father, like every member of the family, was forced to lie still, with his face buried in the carpet.

Suddenly, the shotgun exploded. The father later shared with me that he felt everything was still okay, because the gunman's voice never changed. He continued to speak in measured tones as everyone was told to remain still until they were gone. The father assumed the gunman had simply fired a warning shot into the floor or ceiling. He soon discovered how wrong he was.

As soon as the man left the room, the father and his children witnessed a scene which no human beings should ever have to see. Lying in the floor of her own home, in a pool of blood, was their wife and mother. At point-blank range, the intruder had shot her in the face with a 12-gauge shotgun. So calloused was this criminal, he reflected no emotion whatever in his voice. That she was still alive was nothing short of a miracle. It certainly was not due to the benevolence of the heartless criminal who perpetrated the crime.

She survived the night as a team of experienced doctors worked heroically to save her life. The blast was so close to her son's head, as he huddled against his mother, that his hair was burned. That he too was not seriously wounded or killed is testimony to God's divine protection during the horror.

The shooter was apprehended less than a week later, when he and an accomplice walked up to a man and his wife in the lobby of Bennigan's Restaurant. In broad, open, daylight, they robbed them and then gunned down both of them, as dozens of horrified onlookers watched. The man survived the shooting, but his wife, an accomplished attorney and active volunteer in numerous civic and church organizations, died. For them, the American dream also became an American nightmare.

As information about the shooter became available, an all too familiar story unfolded. The shooter had a long history of criminal activity, including armed robbery, and the use of crack cocaine. In October of 1993, the Texas Parole Board rejected his request for parole from prison, but in mid-November, a federal judge granted him an early release from prison to relieve overcrowding. That was the beginning of a sixty-day crime spree that resulted in at least one death, two more shootings, and several robberies at gunpoint. During his rampage through Houston, the early releasee beat and stomped a pregnant woman, causing serious injuries, including a broken sternum. But at least the criminal did not have to sleep in a crowded prison, thanks to a thoughtful, liberal federal judge.

This lady and her entire family are truly among the most remarkable people I have ever known. Within months of the shooting, the couple was on a mission to stop the early release of violent offenders. She believes her life was spared by a sovereign God, for the purpose of helping to correct some of the injustices of our justice system.

For far too long, the criminal justice system has been dominated by a secular humanist worldview that denies the sinful nature of humanity. In spite of two years of continuing reconstructive surgeries, the wife and mother still bears the scars and visual reminders of her ordeal. That does not deter this brave woman nor her articulate and supportive husband.

One afternoon during the Texas gubernatorial campaign in 1994, I received a call from the couple asking if I could be in their home that evening. The husband explained that George W. Bush, the son of the former president, who was running against Ann Richards for governor, was coming by to see them. That evening, everyone in the room wept as they related their night of terror.

Months later, as Governor of Texas, George Bush returned to Ellington Air Force Base where, with this couple at his side, he signed into law a new crime bill completely restructuring early release to require careful oversight. They are making a difference with their lives.

This whole affair has opened my eyes to a new dimension of injustice that exists in our current, liberal justice system; one that few people even think about until they become a crime victim. While the young thug who marched into their home with a shotgun and started blasting is living comfortably in his air-conditioned cell, receiving free medical and dental treatments, free legal assistance, and free guidance counseling, the victims continue to be victimized.

The night of terror that the "early releasee" perpetrated on their home, transformed their dream house into a house of horrors. Friends of the criminal threatened their children's lives if they testified in court, necessitating a move that resulted in two house payments for months. Their new home included a sophisticated security system, electronic gates, a trained guard dog, and loaded weapons; all in a concentrated effort to restore the feeling of security that their home had once provided. Still, the entire family slept in one room for months before they were able to begin recovering. No one paid for their counseling expenses. Financially, the whole ordeal has been devastating. We have created a system that coddles the criminals and forgets the victims.

A Moral Sinkhole

How did this nation get to the place where criminals feel free to walk into someone's home and start shooting? What is happening to America?

How did we get from Ozzie and Harriet to Beavis and Butthead? How did we get to the moral sinkhole that prevents our courts from being able to decide that the framers of the Constitution were not granting "2 Live Crew" the right to scream the "F" word 226 times, and refer to oral sex eighty-seven times in their recording, "As Nasty As They Wanna Be," when the First Amendment was written? How did we get from cherishing children, to killing one out of every three babies conceived in their mother's womb through abortion? How did we get to the place where we think it wise to prohibit our children from praying in school, while handing out condoms and providing free abortions to seventh graders without parental consent? Clearly something is wrong. In the preceding pages we saw how America was a nation established with a purpose. There is little doubt in the historical record that America was built on Christian principles. We have seen that as our founding fathers sought to obey God and follow His commands, a protective hedge was erected around the nation and great blessings followed. We have embarked on a study of Isaiah 2 and 3, looking at nine detailed prophecies that Isaiah announces will befall any nation that forgets God as He takes away His protective hedge. Now, you will be given a glimpse of how the Christians in Pearland, Texas, a community of 30,000 residents, decided to take a stand for righteousness, and how the influence of those Christians has effected the whole community.

You and I may not be able to change the world, but we can effect change where we are. Born in 1950, I have lived long enough to remember an America where families were intact, God was honored, and people felt safe. I lived through the radical sixties and seventies and witnessed the liberal assault on America. Today, we are witnessing the despair and chaos produced by the bankrupt philosophy of secular humanism and its adherents. It is not too late to recapture the vision and restore the American dream, but the hour is very late.

I am encouraged by recent events in our nation that seem to reflect that God is giving America one more chance to return to moral sanity. The "Promise Keepers" phenomena is clearly something that only God could engineer, and reveals the extent of His love and patience. It also reflects the fact that hundreds of thousands of men in America know that the time has come for men to once again commit themselves to God, their families, and biblical values.

If we are to succeed in returning America to her Christian heritage we must understand that it will not be easy. Pandora's box has been opened. Wrongs are now considered "rights." We face a struggle, but in the end, truth will prevail if men of truth have the courage and determination to assert it. In I Chronicles 12:32, a band of warriors of Issachar joined David. Of them the Scripture states: "...men of Issachar, who understood the times and knew what Israel should do." That is the kind of men America needs today. The men of Issachar said, "Enough is Enough."

For some time now, many of my friends have been urging me to tell the Pearland story. I have been reticent to do so for fear that as I relate the story, I may appear to be exalting myself. Without question, God has done a mighty work in our city, and He is the only one who can continue it. I do not want to jeopardize His blessings.

The Pearland Story

There is a great story to be told and as you read it, my prayer is that you will be encouraged to rise up and, with God's help, change your community. James reminds us in James 4:17, "Anyone who knows the good he ought to do and doesn't do it, sins."

When I moved to Pearland, Texas, in 1990, to pastor First Baptist Church, there was not one member involved in civil government as an elected official at any level. At this writing, three members of our church serve on the city council and all five on the council are professing Christians. Four of our members serve on the school board. The city manager is a member of our church. The police chief is a member of our church. The city attorney is a member of our church. The assistant district attorney of Brazoria County is a member of our church. In addition, our church members serve as volunteers on various committees and commissions throughout our community, county and state.

Pearland is not a Christian community, but Christians are serving in leadership and the decisions they make reflect their convictions and moral commitments. As you read the following pages, you will see that Pearland is prospering because godly people are leading by serving. The scripture instructs us: "When the righteous are in authority, the people rejoice; but when the wicked beareth rule, the people mourn" (Prov. 29:2).

The changes that have come to Pearland did not come easy, nor did they take place overnight, but I can testify they were worth the effort. Satan does not give back occupied territory without a fight, but he will give it back if you stand in the authority of Jesus Christ and say, "Enough is Enough."

"A government is only to be supported by pure religion or austere morals. Private and public virtue is the only foundation of republics."

-John Adams,
2nd President of the United States,
1735 - 1826

Chapter Seventeen

Sex Education or
Sex Indoctrination?

On September 9, 1990, I delivered a message to the members of First Baptist Church, Pearland, Texas, detailing my philosophy of ministry. After 60 days of meetings and various discussions with a very thorough committee of five lay people appointed by the congregation to secure a pastor for the 3,500 member church, I consented to come "in view of a call." In Baptist church polity, a prospective pastor preaches a "trial sermon" to the congregation. If the people like it, they typically accept the recommendation of the Pastor Search Committee, who are expected to do a thorough background work before bringing a recommendation to the church.

I preached a very direct message that addressed how the church would be governed if the congregation chose to extend me an invitation to be their pastor. The four main points of the sermon were; (1) Forgiveness, (2) Fellowship, (3) Finances, and (4) Faith. On each point I attempted to share my philosophy of leadership and my vision for what a church ought to be doing in each area. To my delight, the church embraced my philosophy, voting by a ninety-four percent margin to extend the "call" to me to be their new pastor.

The First Year Was Rewarding

On October 7, 1990, our family became members of First Baptist Church and I formally began my pastoral ministry in Pearland. The first

203

year was both rewarding and challenging. In any new pastorate, there is a period of adjustment. First Baptist had been without a pastor for sixteen months, during which time the entire ministerial staff had resigned. My first order of business was to secure a new staff. During the first month, a dear friend and colaborer, joined me in Pearland to assist in the work. He is like a right arm to me and is one of the most Christlike men I have ever known.

During our first year in Pearland, we baptized 352 and recorded 573 additions. In June of 1991, we voted to find property for the purpose of relocating the entire facility to accommodate expected growth. Everything was moving forward wonderfully.

Throughout the first eighteen months, I preached a number of messages on current event themes, always exhorting our people to be salt and light in the community. In March of 1992, one of our ladies alerted me that a female speaker was going to speak at an assembly program in the high school. Two things about the student assembly bothered her. First, students had to have parental approval to attend the assembly (more about that later). Secondly, the speaker and program was sponsored by the "AIDS Foundation," a very pro-homosexual organization. She requested that I attend the assembly.

The "AIDS Awareness" Assembly

As it worked out, I could not go, due to previously scheduled appointments throughout the day of the assembly, so I sent my associate pastor in my place. Meanwhile, I spent the morning interviewing a prospective staff member. Because Pearland High School, with its 2,200-plus students, has no assembly hall large enough to accommodate the student body, multiple assemblies were scheduled throughout the day.

At about 11:30 a.m., my associate pastor interrupted the interview taking place in my office. He and I have worked together since 1988 and I knew immediately by his countenance that something very disturbing had taken place. At his urging, I decided to conclude the interview and attend the last assembly myself. I arrived at the high school just as the young lady began her remarks and quietly sat down on the back row of the assembly hall. I had the presence of mind to bring my dictaphone with a 30-minute tape which I used to record some of the speaker's remarks.

Many adults equate their own high school experiences to those of today's teenagers, thinking they are the same. That is a mistake. Like automobiles have changed, school has changed, and more than you probably think.

Times Have Changed

I remember the day in the eighth grade when our coach took all the eighth grade boys into the boys' gym where they had taped black paper over the windows. For an hour, we watched vivid depictions of human beings infected with various forms of venereal disease. When the lights came back on, there was little doubt in our minds that our parents, pastors and teachers were correct; sexual promiscuity had grave consequences. Some still engaged in it, but no one left that assembly able to truthfully say they were never warned. That was considered an assembly on venereal disease in the mid '60s. No one dared to suggest that sexual behavior before marriage or beyond marriage was acceptable, and adults never considered showing such explicit material to a mixed audience. Had someone implied it was acceptable to engage in sexual activity outside of marriage, they would have been fired summarily.

That has all changed in the '90s. I listened to a cute, petite, bubbly, twenty-four-year-old coed speak to our students, including my own daughter, Misty, who sat midway in the auditorium. I could not believe my ears. She spoke in the vernacular of her audience, using just enough technical terms to alert everyone that she knew what she was talking about. She proceeded to describe in great detail every form of sexual expression you can imagine. She used humor to diffuse the tension and embarrassment that a mixed crowd of teenagers would feel, as various sexual activities were vividly described. She was careful **not** to pass moral judgment on any behavior.

I was able to constrain my inner feelings as she described normal intercourse, anal sex, and oral sex, which she announced to be the safest way to have sex in the world of AIDS, outside of masturbation, that is. Predictably, she displayed a condom, today's amoral solution for the host of afflictions that accompany illicit sex. She stretched it, made jokes about the male anatomy, and announced, "Condoms are ninety-seven percent effective in combating AIDS when used correctly. I cannot describe to you how incensed I was as I listened to this young lady. She was giving license to hundreds of students, including two of my own, who were in high school at the time, to commit any wicked act they chose. To now add to her shame, her purported fact that condoms were ninety-seven percent safe in preventing AIDS, was more than I could take. I had had "Enough."

Questionable Information

I quickly raised my hand. She politely recognized my inquiry, doubtlessly assuming I was a teacher or administrator. You can imagine the expression on my daughter's face when she heard her preacher-father's voice ring throughout the room. The entire assembly gasped to realize the Baptist preacher was present.

"Ma'am," I asked, "Where did you get your statistics of ninety-seven percent? I have read a lot on the subject, but I have never heard anyone suggest condoms were ninety-seven percent safe." Putting this in perspective, can you imagine an airline running an ad campaign that announces excitedly that only three out of every one hundred of their passengers, that fly their airline, die in a crash? Only in the wicked minds of those who are determined to defy God's laws, regarding fornication, is this kind of reasoning considered acceptable. When it comes to drinking, we tell kids to "just say no" or "think before you drink." When it comes to smoking, we say "You can't, we won't let you." But when it comes to illicit sex, which the humanists themselves apparently cannot live without, 3 dying out of every 100 is an acceptable price to pay.

The young lady now realized I was not a friend. She tortly snapped, "The CDC," and proceeded on with her discussions.

I raised my hand again, and suddenly every eye in the room turned in my direction, most with a look of contempt. At first, she chose to ignore me, but I am a rather persistent person. When it became obvious that I was not going to be denied, she finally acknowledged me again. "Ma'am," I began, "I have read a lot of material on condoms released from the Center for Disease Control, in Atlanta, Georgia. (I wanted her to know I knew her abbreviations.) Are you sure of your statistic? I have never known of anyone claiming condoms are ninety-seven percent effective." From across the room, one of the teachers shouted that she had read the same statistic. I knew she had not, but it was obvious this was not the time nor place to continue the discussion. The main reason I interrupted her to start with was to make sure that those two hundred and fifty, or more, students, including my own daughter, knew that not everyone present agreed with the immoral presentation they were hearing, and that the facts being offered were not necessarily correct. When I approached the speaker following the program, she acknowledged she had exaggerated the statistic.

As the students filed out of the room, I experienced quite a bit of hostility from some who thought I was being mean to the speaker. After all, we discovered after she and I exchanged words, she herself was HIV-positive. She informed the students that she was able to continue having sex because she herself used condoms, and she believed in their safety. As liberals often do, she concluded with an emotional appeal, asserting, "I am dying of AIDS (she has since expired), but I am here because I care about you." To this day, I wonder how many kids she added to the rolls of the HIV-positive ranks, by her assembly at Pearland High School.

"Daddy, I Am So Proud Of You"

There were several students who thanked me for standing up and speaking out, but one meant more than all the others. My daughter, who would graduate later that semester, walked over to me, threw her arms around my neck, and said, "Daddy, I am so proud of you." Tears fill my eyes as I recount that moment. No one will ever be able to take that moment away from me. That was just the beginning of a war that was soon to follow.

That afternoon, after checking with an attorney to clarify any legal issues, I decided to transcribe the assembly content from the tape I had recorded and make copies available to the citizens of Pearland. Our church is located on a major artery on the southeast side of Houston where thousands of cars pass each day. I displayed on our large marquee out front "Learn what students heard about AIDS this Sunday." You can imagine what a stir that created in our community.

A Packed Church House

Sunday, the church was packed, just as I expected. What I did not anticipate was a reporter from the Houston Chronicle showing up. At the conclusion of my message, I announced to the congregation that we would dismiss for a ten-minute recess, after which, we would reconvene. This would allow an opportunity for anyone not interested in hearing a discussion on the AIDS assembly to leave. Very few did.

That morning I read the entire twelve-page document to our church family and friends, including the Chronicle reporter. Our senior ladies heard their pastor say words, I am certain, they never expected to hear him say. I decided if our kids could hear them, their parents and grandparents needed to hear them. That day, the members of First Baptist Church of Pearland decided "Enough was Enough."

I left town early the next day to escape the media onslaught that followed. I had requests from numerous news agencies for interviews, which I declined. I finally granted one interview to a supportive interviewer in Austin, Texas. My intent was to assure the controversial assembly remained a Pearland issue and that the media not be allowed to turn it into a circus.

The School Board Meeting

I requested the privilege of addressing the next school board meeting. Needless to say, it was well-attended. In fact, it was moved twice before a location big enough to accommodate the crowd was found. I was told between 500-600 people were in attendance. The overwhelming majority were from our congregation.

Until that evening, always excusing myself by thinking I was just too busy, I had never attended any public meetings in Pearland, whether school board or city council. I soon received quite an education in politics. School board policy required that a person had to request the privilege of speaking to the board prior to the meeting. I discovered that of the seven requests to address the board that evening, I was the only one speaking in opposition to the AIDS assembly. Other speakers included faculty members, one student, a faculty member's husband, and another pastor in our community.

Interestingly, I was first, which I found to be suspicious in that I was the only one in opposition to the assembly. I was spiritually and mentally prepared for that evening, having spent days in seclusion alone with God. The assumption, by many present, was that the "Baptist preacher" would storm in, asserting his own, narrow-minded, Victorian, repressive, antisex education views.

The "God Factor"

I cannot prove it, but there appeared to be a plan to then send six consecutive reasoned and passionate speakers, with a broad range of perspectives, to refute the "Baptist preacher." What no one from the opposing viewpoint considered was the "God Factor."

In "Chariots of Fire," one of Hollywood's commendable achievements, the thrilling story of Eric Liddell is told. Eric Liddell refused to run the 100-yard dash, for which he trained for years, in the 1924 Olympics, because the qualifying heats were conducted on Sunday. His Christian commitment prohibited him from running on Sunday. Instead, he entered the 440, a race most sprinters are ill-equipped to run. No one gave him a chance.

In the movie, an American runner walked up to Eric, who was running under Great Britain's flag, and gave him a note. It read, "God honors those that honor Him," a paraphrase of I Samuel 2:30. Eric amazingly won the race, and achieved his gold medal. He later died serving his God in China as a foreign missionary. It was no accident that long after his death, a Hollywood producer stumbled onto the story of his life and produced a movie that became an Academy Award-winning motion picture. Today, over seventy years later, God is still honoring a young man who honored Him. That's what I mean by the "God Factor."

Addressing The School Board

When I stood to speak, I began by praising the faculty and administration for their commitment to our children. I thanked them for caring enough about our young people to schedule outside speakers to address the AIDS epidemic which threatens the lives of so many. I assured them that I was not against sex education, when offered from a Judeo-Christian perspective that properly emphasizes abstinence as the only truly safe approach.

I then began to address my concerns with the recent assembly. I purposefully spoke softly, avoided any personal references, and made a conscientious effort not to use divisive terms. I did, however, speak directly to my moral concerns regarding what I believed to be a direct attack on prevailing community standards. I objected to the vulgar language used in the assembly, and the blatantly wrong and misleading information. I delivered a well-constructed and factual presentation that was interrupted repeatedly by applause, including two separate standing ovations. When I sat down, I sensed God's pleasure. One of the first people I remember expressing support, outside my incredible wife, was Pearland's lone African-American minister. He and I soon became close friends. My children, staff, and church family were equally supportive and encouraging.

The next six speakers spoke as if they had not heard one thing I had said. They attempted to refute positions that I had just clarified I did not hold, particularly that of being "anti" sex education. The other minister had been invited to speak because he is well-respected and greatly loved in our community. It became clear to me that he was being used to bolster an indefensible position. I did not know him well at the time, but I was amazed that he could justify defending something that I believed to be so clearly wrong. I was embarrassed for him and shamed for the cause of Christ. As a result of his speaking, I did something for which I am ashamed. I assumed that he was my enemy and labeled him as a typical liberal intellectual, not unlike so many I had encountered in seminary and while traveling around the country. It wasn't long until God taught me an invaluable lesson about judging others. That same pastor is now among my closest friends, and a man I hold in high esteem. (More about that later.)

Good Things Started Happening

As a result of this whole episode, a number of good things came to pass. We discovered that while the principal of the high school attempted to defend the assembly on the grounds that the students were required to obtain permission to attend, the high school's means of implementation was deceptive. The method that was employed was to state that if you did not want your son or daughter to attend such an activity, you had to respond in writing. That meant, if your son or daughter never mentioned the event and you did not respond because you did not know about it, you gave your approval. That policy has been changed and the principal that allowed the assembly is no longer employed by the Pearland Independent School District. The school board employed a new principal that has endeared himself to both students and parents since he arrived. Last year he served as chairman of our youth committee for Pearland's first, ever, citywide crusade. In addition, with the aid and support of our superintendent and principal, in 1994 the Pearland Ministerial Alliance sponsored Pearland's first baccalaureate service in over twenty years. It is now an annual event.

Christians are now involved in politics. Almost immediately after these events, two of our members, with my encouragement, ran for the school board. They were both elected. We now have four members from our church serving on the school board. This past spring, we had the unique circumstance of two of our members, both wonderfully committed to our kids, running for the same position. When they wound up in a runoff election against each other, I asked them to stand up on Sunday morning and said, "choose one."

We still have assemblies. Since our new principal arrived, the students have been shown a videotape of a popular Spring Branch teacher who contracted AIDS and subsequently died. His story is riveting. He, like the previous AIDS speaker, kept the attention of the kids, but not with distasteful, crude humor. Rather, he revealed the sobering and staggering facts about AIDS and how illicit sex was going to cost him his life. He told the agonizing details of his struggle with AIDS. He presented one message about sex: wait until marriage. Our sex education curriculum offered at Pearland High School now stresses the importance of abstinence, and warns of the consequences of promiscuity. Interestingly enough, in July of 1995, the Federal Drug Administration released a report finally admitting that the HIV virus is so small that it often passes right through microscopic holes in many latex condoms. Amazingly, they still refuse to admit that abstinence until marriage is the only safe approach to sex.

Perhaps the most important thing that happened during this important confrontation with the school system was that I realized the importance of the church being involved in the community. I have discovered that many people who love their country, love their children, and love their God, have devoted their lives to public service. They often feel abandoned by the church. The only time they hear from Christians is when the Christian community is upset about something they have done, or been accused of doing. We Christians are known more by what we are against than what we are for. That is a reality that we must correct. I have discovered many great public servants who had been quietly serving in our community for many years.

New Days Necessitate New Ways

Perhaps it is time for the Church to reevaluate the way we define service. I returned to the pastorate in 1988 after fourteen years in evangelism. I have come to the conviction that the evangelical church is going to have to assess what we require of our people if we are going to effectively change our world for Christ. We have allowed a paradigm to become rooted in our midst that is counterproductive. I know what I am about to say is true in the church culture that I have known all my life. I suspect it's true in every major organized church culture in America.

We evaluate a person's depth of commitment to Christ based on how often he attends our church programs. If he shows any spiritual depth, or even potential depth, we place him in a leadership role. For Southern Baptist churches, that typically means Sunday morning Bible study class, followed by congregation worship, Sunday evening church training, followed by another congregational worship time, and Wednesday evening Bible study. Add to that, outreach on Monday night and choir rehearsal on yet another evening, workdays, special events, etc., for the most dedicated of our members (at least by our standard of measurement), and what you have is an exhausted Christian with nothing left to give.

These same people are juggling PTO meetings, ball practice, piano lessons, gymnastics, and homework around a forty and fifty hour workweek. No wonder many Christians, who are also citizens, have withdrawn from public service. In their absence, a very small number of non-Christians, including those with radical anti-Christian agendas, have been able to control and manipulate the civil politics of America with little or no opposition. Today, many Christians do not even vote.

To evangelize an increasingly pagan culture today, the Church must get back into the civil arena. We must find ways to provide adequate discipleship and Christian growth, while freeing Christians to participate in public policy areas where their Christian influence can be applied and their witness can become effective. We may need less "gathered" church, and more "scattered" church, if we are going to make a difference. The mentality of withdrawing to our church fortresses, while the world is marching toward destruction must be changed. Christians must let their light shine.

In Pearland, no political civil body meets without Christians being involved. An AIDS assembly motivated the Christians in Pearland to say, "Enough is Enough." The scripture again proves true:

"And we know that in all things God works for the good of those who love him, who have been called according to his purpose" (Romans 8:28).

"History fails to record a single precedent in which nations subject to moral decay have not passed into political and economic decline. There has been either a spiritual awakening to overcome the moral lapse, or a progressive deterioration leading to ultimate national disaster."

-General Douglas MacArthur

Chapter Eighteen

Mobilizing The Ministerial Alliance

Shortly after arriving in Pearland, I received a call from a fellow pastor in the community who invited me to attend the monthly Ministerial Alliance meeting, held on the first Thursday of every month, at the Golfcrest Country Club. I attended the next meeting, and though I enjoyed the fellowship, I was not very impressed. It basically amounted to a monthly get-together, partially underwritten by the mayor of our city through his business. With the demands of trying to pastor a growing church, I did not view attending the Ministerial Alliance meetings as a top priority. I rarely attended during the next eighteen months.

In May of 1992, the same month of the school board elections in which two of our members were elected to the school board, President Bush declared a National Day of Prayer and Fasting. In April, I called one of the identified leaders of the Ministerial Alliance and discussed the importance of our local pastors declaring a local observance of prayer, in keeping with the request of our president. I was informed that would be impossible, because it fell on the same day as "our monthly noon luncheon at the country club."

The National Day of Prayer and Fasting

The irony of not being able to observe a National Day of Prayer and Fasting because it interrupted a luncheon meeting did not strike me as being funny. I politely hung up and redialed the local papers to initiate sponsoring the observance on the steps of city hall through our church. I contacted the mayor, city council, school board members, and school administrative officials, and the city manager and his staff. I received universal endorsement of the idea. I then wrote members of the Ministerial Alliance and invited them to participate.

Over 100 officials and laypeople attended Pearland's first formal observance of the National Day of Prayer and Fasting. It has since become an annual event with many of the pastors in the city participating. Our police chief, who is a gifted musician and committed Christian, led us in music and various pastors led in prayer. It was a wonderful event. Many of our civic leaders expressed their appreciation for the "Ministerial Alliance" sponsoring such an event.

I was surprised to discover that their perception was that the Ministerial Alliance had sponsored the event, but nevertheless, overjoyed with the response. As my staff loaded up the sound equipment we provided, I decided to go to the Ministerial Alliance luncheon, which had been rescheduled for 1:00 p.m. Once I arrived, several pastors were very cool toward me. As I went through the buffet line, three pastors approached me to discuss the noon events. Whether they appointed themselves or were sent by the others, I have never bothered to ask.

Who Do You Think You Are?

The pastor who had opposed me before the school board one month earlier, spoke for the group. They were demanding by what authority I had assumed the right to schedule an event in the name of the Ministerial Alliance. As you read this, please remember that the AIDS assembly school board meeting was still very fresh on everyone's mind. Already more than a little miffed at their spokesman, I erupted. He and I decided to move the discussions to my office.

The meeting was tenuous to say the least, but to his great credit, the pastor heard me out. He accepted my explanation that I never intended to imply that the Ministerial Alliance, as a body, was hosting the noon prayer time. He understood how local leaders would naturally assume that the pastors in our city had sponsored the event which spiritually impacted a number of people significantly.

We then discussed our differences regarding the school assembly. At first, we got nowhere. Then I asked him if he had ever read a copy of the assembly? To my surprise, he had not. As I waited, he began reading, and the more he read, the more embarrassed he became. Like me regarding him, he had preconceived notions about the "Baptist" preacher. That day God began removing barriers that existed between two very different pastors. Judgmentalism takes many forms and wears many faces, but it is always divisive and destructive.

When he finished reading the assembly transcript, he asked my forgiveness. I embraced him as my friend that day, but I told him; "Your repentance will not be complete until you apologize before this whole community." He assured me he would pray about it and our meeting ended.

A New President

Shortly after that meeting, I received a call from the Afro-American pastor who had stood with me when I addressed the school board. He implored me to return to the Ministerial Alliance meetings. He informed me that he had just been elected president of the fellowship and under his guidance, the Mnisterial Alliance was going to be involved in the city. I remembered his support during the battle with the school board and determined that I owed him my support in return.

He is to be commended for the visionary leadership he has provided in our city. Several innovative measures were undertaken during the next thirty months, including "leadership meetings" sponsored by the Ministerial Alliance. Local civil leaders were invited to a luncheon and breakfast, where issues of concern could be discussed, followed by a message from God's Word. He and I shared a common vision that the church should provide moral leadership in every arena of life.

A Public Apology

Throughout 1993, the fellowship among the various pastors in Pearland grew closer and closer as we got to know each other. We discovered we had more in common than we thought. Then one day, the pastor whom I had been at odds with called me in my study and instructed me to read his weekly article in the *Pearland Journal*. What I read humbled me and endeared this fellow pastor to my heart, as he publicly apologized for opposing me before the school board.

I believe this public apology, more than any other single factor, opened the door for God to send a revival to Pearland. In the months to follow, we witnessed a miracle that impacted city hall, the school system, the churches and the community. *When God moves, He really moves.*

The Pearland Ministerial Alliance has continued to mature, providing moral and spiritual leadership in our city. In 1993, we were requested by the city to officially participate in the Pearland Centennial Celebration by hosting an event during 1994. We chose to sponsor a citywide crusade which we dubbed, "The Pearland Centennial Crusade." Nineteen of our twenty-two churches participated in the July, 1994, crusade. International Evangelist, Jay Strack was invited to speak as hundreds filled the Pearland High School football stadium. By week's end, more than 300 commitments to Christ were recorded.

The Centennial Crusade

Perhaps the most significant events took place prior to the crusade. Through the efforts of hundreds of Christians, members of various churches gathered together each month for prayer meetings, youth rallies, and banquets. Many long-term friendships took on a new dimension, as Christians of all faiths rallied to a common cause of lifting up Jesus for our community to see. On Friday night, preceding the first crusade service on Sunday evening, more than one hundred believers of all faiths participated in an all-night prayer meeting at the football stadium. My laypeople still comment occasionally about the impact of witnessing their pastor, walking arm in arm with two other pastors, as we marched around the stadium track just before dawn, singing, praying and praising God for his mighty dealings in our city.

Vic Coppinger, our beloved mayor and my dear friend, died of cancer on March 28, 1995. Two pastors and myself were all invited to participate, along with his pastor, in the funeral ceremony. I saw Vic weep during the all-night prayer meeting as he saw the churches working together to exalt Jesus over Pearland.

I am not so naive as to suggest that all the churches ought to come together and drop their doctrinal distinctives. I have serious doctrinal disagreements with some in our Ministerial Alliance over various church beliefs, as they do with me. We have made a conscious decision in Pearland to rally around our agreements. We can agree to exalt Christ, call men to repentance, and stand together on common moral issues. We can accomplish far more together than we can alone.

Today, Pearland is a better community because the pastors have sought to stand together, against sin and for righteousness. No longer do the civic leaders make major decisions that effect the citizens of Pearland without first consulting the pastors of the local congregations. They still make the decisions, but they now recognize that pastors can provide valuable guidance and important assistance for their policies. The Ministerial Alliance has become "salt and light," in Pearland, and when we need to, we stand up and say, "Enough is Enough."

"Providence has showered, on this favored land, blessings without number, and has chosen you as the guardians of freedom, to preserve it for the benefit of the human race."

-President Andrew Jackson
March 4, 1837

Chapter Nineteen

Politics, Passions And People Getting Involved

On November 30, 1990, a lieutenant retired from the Houston Police Department after twenty-one years of active duty. On December 1, 1990, the retired Lieutenant, Mike Hogg, was named chief of police in Pearland, Texas. Officer Hogg came to Pearland with a sterling reputation in law enforcement. While with the HPD he spent five years with the vice squad and three years with the elite Special Weapons And Tactics Team (SWAT Team). The new chief quickly endeared himself with the residents of Pearland, working tirelessly with area civic clubs, schools, and Pearland churches, promoting the police department and serving the people.

I was immediately attracted to the new chief because of his transparent love and commitment to Christ. A gifted soloist, Chief Hogg sang in churches throughout the community and often lead music for churches when their minister of music was away.

A Move To Dismiss The Chief

On June 21, 1993, word circulated throughout the community that Chief Hogg was in danger of being dismissed as Pearland police chief by the city council. Upon inquiry, I was informed that a group of city council members wanted to remove him, and that he was subject to being reviewed at the next city council meeting. On June 21, I attended my first-ever city council meeting, along with more than 200 other citizens,

221

about half of them from First Baptist Church. The chief was accompanied by his attorney, a well-known specialist on governmental affairs. He knew well the inner workings of governmental politics, having served as the first assistant to the Harris County district attorney, before entering private practice.

When the city council realized that the chief had broad public support in the community, they very wisely decided to postpone any action that evening. When the public discovered that Chief Hogg had prepared a written response to the charges that were being leveled against him, the audience demanded that he be allowed to address the council. Reluctantly, the council consented.

Chief Hogg did not just read a statement. He read an indictment of the behavior of the actions of most of the council members. His twenty-page statement was an education in local Pearland politics for most of us. The longer he read, the more determined I became to stand with him. Virtue, honesty and courage are in increasingly short supply among public servants, and I saw all of those qualities in our police chief. When he concluded his remarks you could see the measured anger in the eyes of his accusers, though they joined the crowd who wildly applauded the chief.

Several people, including myself, spoke public words of commendation and support of the chief, but one man stood out above the rest. Rather than looking up to the council members in their raised chairs, this gentleman turned and faced the crowd and began to speak. In no uncertain terms, he informed us that the folks behind him were all politicians, and the one thing all politicians did well, was count votes. He proceeded to assure us that as soon as the citizenry settled down, the council would fire the police chief. I was impressed to discover that the speaker was himself an elected official. I added the justice of the peace to my growing list of local heroes.

A Move To Dismiss The City Manager

I determined that evening that I would not abandon our chief. Within days, word again circulated of a potential firing at city hall. This time the target was our city manager. It seems that the council members decided that he was responsible for the public humiliation they had received during the June meeting. They deduced that if the city manager had fired the police chief as they had previously suggested, the June meeting would have never happened. They decided to start the proceedings of removing our new city manager, whom they had hired the previous year.

Though at the time, I was uninformed concerning local Pearland politics, I soon discovered that city managers did not last long in our small city. I found their tenure of service closely resembled that of most Baptist pastors. The existing city manger was Pearland's third in four years.

The July 21, 1993, edition of the *Pearland Journal* reported that one of our council members moved to instruct the city attorney to inquire into the propriety of a settlement that our city manager had negotiated on behalf of the city with certain city employees regarding compensation for overtime. A second council member seconded the motion. It carried 5-0.

On the heels of that motion, a third council member moved that the council give the city manager a vote of confidence for his role in the negotiations. After much discussion, the *Journal* reported that one of the council members stated "council keeps beating around the bush and needs to decide if this man is going to be the city manager or not." The council adjourned without voting on the motion to give the city manager a vote of confidence.

A Divided City Council

From this meeting, clear divisions in our city council began surfacing. The divisions became more distinct in the months to come. Our mayor identified himself staunchly behind our city manager, along with one council member. Three other members clearly identified themselves as opponents of the city manager. The fifth council member made a valiant effort in the early stages of the controversy to stay neutral and paid a great price for his neutrality.

The meeting closed at 11:29 p.m. without any action being taken. It was determined that at the next council meeting, the results of an annual evaluation of the city manager would be released to the public and a decision regarding his future employment would be made at that time.

The July twenty-third edition of the *Pearland Journal* announced that "On Monday, July 26, the city council will vote on the future of the city, or so say a lot of citizens of Pearland." Upon reading such statements and hearing increasing reports of the division that existed in our city government, I remembered my commitment to stay involved.

Mixing Religion And Politics

A growing number of our church family felt uncomfortable with their pastor "mixing religion and politics." Believing that religion ought to be mixed with everything, I informed our congregation on Sunday evening that an important called city council meeting to discuss the employment of our city manager, had been scheduled for the following evening, July 26, at the unusual hour of 5:30 p.m.

That evening, a standing room only crowd attended the city council meeting. Just one week before, a majority of the members of the city council were discussing the dismissal of Pearland's third city manager in less than 3 years. Suddenly, with a packed council chamber, accented by a number of representatives from the local news media, the council had a change of heart. (Reminiscent of the sudden reversal during the police chief's inquisition, the month before.)

That evening, eleven citizens spoke on behalf of the city manager, including myself. Like the chief, our city manager secured a well-known attorney to represent him, and prepared a lengthy statement for the council. Several members of the council wanted to go into executive session, but the city manager requested a public hearing.

After an impressive review of accomplishments during his first year as our city manager, he stated, "I deserve to keep my job. I feel my record speaks for itself...I both live and work with enthusiasm. I am a devoted Christian who holds my conviction above my personal welfare. I am a good daddy, a faithful husband, a patriotic American, a compassionate and loyal friend and as Jesus taught, a good servant. A servant who can and will make Pearland a better place to live."

A New Hero

When the city manager completed his remarks, I added the name of Paul Grohman to my list of heroes. I was in the process of discovering that many very fine people enter the field of public service for all the right reasons. Unfortunately, they get thrown aside by unscrupulous politicians and the failure of decent citizens to support them. Neither the city manager nor the police chief are perfect people. They, like you and I, grapple with personal flaws and failures every day. Since 1993, they have been meeting with me on a weekly basis to study God's Word and pray together. They have become very close friends. I determined that Pearland needed people of their caliber in leadership. Their own public testimonies help mobilize the Christian community. That night, the city council voted to postpone discussing Paul Grohman's future employment as manager of the City of Pearland for ninety days. The citizens won a battle that night, but the war was just beginning.

More Controversy

On Thursday of that week, July 29, 1993, the *Houston Chronicle* broke a story of alleged illegalities involving the Pearland City Council. The Brazoria County grand jury was convened to hear allegations that the Pearland City Council violated the Texas Open Meetings Act and that one council member received illegal compensation from the city. The following article carried in the Pearland Journal, August 4, 1993, details the allegations against the council member:

The Brazoria County grand jury will meet this week to hear the allegations that a Pearland City Council member received funds illegally as compensation for his post.

Pearland city council members receive $250 per month. According to a ruling by the State Attorney General, (name withheld), council member for three years, received compensation in violation of the state law. In that ruling it states "state employees or other individuals who receive all or part of their compensation directly or indirectly from funds of the State of Texas and who are not State officers, shall not be barred from service as members of the governing body of school districts, cities, town, or other local governmental districts; provided however, that such state employees or other individuals shall receive no salary for serving as members of such governing bodies."

(Name withheld) is the department chairman of Alvin Community College's criminal justice training center. He acknowledged receiving $9,000, but repaid the amount when he learned of the ruling.

Documents indicate that City Attorney Lester Rorick sent (name withheld) a letter on June 10, 1991 warning his acceptance of a $250 monthly salary violated state law. Rorick said because the college receives state funds, at least part of (name withheld) salary was being paid directly or indirectly by those funds, which makes him ineligible for compensation as a council member.

On June 17, 1991, (name withheld) requested the then-City Manager, Jim DeShaser to remove him from the city's compensation list.

However, on July 21, 1992, (name withheld) sent another letter asking City Manager Paul Grohman to place his name back on the list. Compensation was paid until July 12, 1993 when (name withheld), on advice from his attorney, returned the money and asked that his name be removed from the list.

(Name withheld) said in a published report that he felt the allegations against him are politically motivated by city officials.

The District Attorney's office will also hear allegations that Pearland City Council violated the Texas Open Meetings Act. Assistant District Attorney Tom Selleck said in a telephone conversation that he really doesn't know what those charges are until he hears it from the grand jury.

He said he received certain allegations of the council's agenda not being posted properly and there were some items which were not discussed.

Selleck said he received calls from "concerned citizens' " on the matter.

Mayor Vic Coppinger said he cannot comment until he learns what these charges are.

At a recent meeting, Coppinger said he had been advised not to sign the minutes of a closed session which cited the violations.

The grand jury will meet on Wednesday. [110]

Remarkably, the Grand Jury "No Billed" the council member. This was my first encounter with what I believe to have been injustice at the county level. On September 7, 1993, citizens submitted a recall petition, requesting a recall election on three council members. The petitions contained more than twice the number of signatures required to force a recall, but on September 11, the petitions were returned. The city secretary ruled they were incomplete and therefore, invalid. This maneuver served to further galvanize a core of citizens in their effort to unseat the three council members.

Corrected petitions were presented a second time to the city council, but again disqualified by the city secretary on technical grounds. That same week, the chief of police wrote an editorial featured in both the local newspapers, calling the city to prayer. He led in a prayer vigil at Independence Park on September 27.

In the midst of all of this, on September 15, the *Pearland Journal* reported that the city attorney was abruptly fired by a three-to-two council vote. Three council members voted in a block for dismissal. In the same meeting, all three voted to hire another attorney, despite one council member acknowledging never having heard of the attorney.

Citizens Sued

On October 6, 1993, two major news stories broke in the press. New petitions, gathered in less than seven days, were submitted to the city secretary, seeking a recall election for the council members who had repeatedly voted in unison. In the same newspaper, it was announced that those same three council members had filed suit against nine citizens, alleging that the recall petitions were libelous. Three more citizens were added to the lawsuit later.

We soon discovered that across America, citizens were increasingly being sued by the elected representatives for speaking out against them. There have been so many lawsuits filed in recent years, a new acronym has been coined to describe the suits: "SLAPP" or Strategic Lawsuits Against Public Participation. You can imagine the chilling effects such lawsuits have in a community. Twelve citizens in our community have had to expend thousands of dollars of their own money to cover their legal expenses to defend their right to exercise their freedom of speech. After more than $12,000 of expenses, nine citizens were later dropped from the lawsuit. Three are still in litigation as of this writing.

For the next two months, the battle at City Hall raged on, with each council meeting becoming more bitter and each side leveling new charges. The recall election was scheduled for December 11. At noon, on Monday, November 11, 1993, the District Judge in the 149th District Court of Brazoria County, granted an injunction to halt the recall election of December 11. The judge ruled the petitions failed to meet the criterion required in the City Charter regarding specific charges against the officials.

One of those present at the hearing stated, "The judge made his decision without benefit of testimony and without examining the prepared evidence." That was my second encounter with injustice in Brazoria County.

A Time For Action

On December 1, 1993, I decided it was time to take a bold public action. Fully aware of the propensity of some council members to sue citizens, I published a major statement in both Pearland papers entitled, "A Time For Action." The reaction to the statement was predictable. Convinced that the stalemate in our city had to be broken, I elected to speak out. It was obvious to all, by that time, that justice would be difficult to obtain in Brazoria County. I publicly called one member of our city council to resign. A portion of my open letter is reprinted below:

Our city government has been in turmoil for the past twelve months and I believe it is time for it to come to an end. It is time for the citizenry to stand up and be counted.

Since then, Paul Grohman, has been constantly harassed and hindered from doing his job. Our city has made headlines regularly for the division on our council (always 3-2). Two petitions have been circulated, signed by more than the necessary residents to force a recall election, only to be tossed aside on technicalities. 12 citizens have been sued, (an effort to intimidate through lengthy and expensive legal maneuvers) valuable time and opportunity for progress has been wasted and the abuse of power continues.

If we capitulate and allow these injustices to go unanswered, at the expense of faithful and capable city employees like Mike Hogg and Paul Grohman who have courageously stood up to the "Good Ole Boy" system that has dominated this city for 30 years, God will give us exactly what we deserve.

Remember: "Scornful men bring a city into a snare" (Proverbs 29:8). [111]

Men's Retreat At Trinity Pines Baptist Encampment

In February, eighty of our men accompanied their pastor to Trinity Pines Baptist Encampment for a men's retreat. I elected to speak, foregoing a guest speaker, which we routinely bring in for such retreats. On Saturday afternoon, I put a chalkboard in front of our men and made the bold declaration. "In May, two positions on the city council will become vacant. Today, you will either name at least one of our congregation to run for city council...or I am personally running." They knew I would.

Two hours later, one name surfaced as the clear choice, above several very qualified individuals. The man they chose is perhaps the most transparent Christian I have ever known. Politics was not even a consideration as far as he was concerned, but as in all things, he consented to pray about the matter. Two weeks later, prepared to tell his pastor "No," God moved in his heart through the sermon that day, and when we met, the choice of the men said "Yes." In May of 1994, a coalition of Christians and concerned citizens with common moral concerns, fielded two candidates, both committed Christians. Both men were elected on the first ballot. In one election, the city council moved from a 3-2 majority against our mayor and city manager, to a 4-1 majority for them.

Then in May of 1995, another dedicated Christian and member of First Baptist Church, Pearland, was elected by acclamation, running without opposition. Today, five committed Christians serve on the city council in Pearland, Texas. "What about the council member who sought to remain neutral," you ask?

A Great Story

I believe that council member's story is the most encouraging aspect of this whole episode. During the height of the controversy swirling around the talk of dismissing our city manager, I felt compelled to go to this council member's home. I perceived that he was sincerely seeking to do what was right, yet he was vacillating on whether or not to retain our city manager due to the controversies. That evening, God enabled me to look inside that council member's heart. I left there believing in my spirit that we would continue to disagree on some issues, but that he and his wife were Christians and that they wanted to do what was right.

In the days to come, he and I strongly disagreed on a number of issues publicly. Increasingly, he became identified with everything many of us felt was wrong in Pearland politics. His positions were opposed by many citizens, which discredited him greatly in the eyes of many. When the showdown at city hall finally came, he withdrew his support for the dismissal of the city manager, but the damage had been done.

You can imagine our collective surprise when on a Sunday in the Summer of 1994, that same council member and his family showed up in our church services. Everyone felt a little clumsy, in light of recent political events, but after about the third visit, Tommye and I invited him and his wife out to dinner. We thoroughly enjoyed our time together. Over the next two months, it became obvious to everyone that God was doing something that superseded politics. In September of 1994, Randy Weber and his two sons were baptized into our fellowship. His wife, Brenda, and their daughter joined by statement of their faith, having been previously baptized. He and his family are among our most faithful members, and today I count him as one of my closest friends. The testimony of this family reminds all of us at First Baptist Church that when you stand up for what is right, God will honor your witness and make even your enemies be at peace with you (Proverbs 16:7). To God be the glory. The following is a portion of a letter that Councilman Weber recently wrote to both Pearland papers:

Thanks to (name withheld) for standing up amidst all the

turmoil over our city manager. Because he and our late mayor took the stand they took, they kept us from making a terrible mistake. Because I had listened to false information, I was about to make a bad mistake in joining a vote to fire Paul Grohman.

With a new council now, my prayer is that Pearland will truly heal and be an example for many other cities. I was wrong in my belief that Paul Grohman was out to "do the council in." I admit it.

Casey Jones was right in his article when he said I should ask for the city manager's forgiveness and we should show the world two Christians working together. I have asked for his forgiveness and can only pray that in time (his wife) will forgive me, too. A few scriptures from Proverbs to consider:

"Hatred stirs up strife, but love covers all offenses" (Prov. 10:12).

"By the blessing of the upright a city is exalted, but it is overthrown by the mouth of the wicked" (Proverbs 11:11).

"A soft answer turns away wrath, but a harsh word stirs up anger" (Proverbs 15:1).

"For lack of wood the fire goes out; and where there is no whisperer, quarreling ceases" (Proverbs 26:20).

"Scoffers set a city aflame, but wise men turn away wrath" (Proverbs 29:8).

How about it, (council members)? Look where we are as a community?

Aren't we in better shape than ever? I believe that most people would say we are, and if you would really do some soul searching, I think you would have to admit so, too.

Can't we admit our mistake...? [112]

Today, Pearland is prospering because citizens and elected officials have stood together and said, "Enough is Enough." In 1994, when the President's Crime Bill allocated money for local municipalities to fight crime, Pearland did not qualify. Our crime rate was too low. We believe God has raised a hedge around our city.

"The Church must take right grounds in regards to politics...the time has come for Christians to vote for honest men, and take consistent ground in politics or the Lord will curse them."

-Evangelist Charles Finney (1792-1875)

Chapter Twenty

The Pastors' Roundtable

During the 1992 congressional and presidential election campaigns, I received an invitation to attend a breakfast meeting of the Southeast Texas Pastors' Roundtable held each month. I decided to attend. That is when I met Steve Stockman whom I learned was running for the congressional seat which Jack Brooks had occupied since 1952.

I liked Steve from the start. He is one of the most optimistic men you will ever meet. How else do you explain a total political novice, with no support base, no finances, and no endorsements, taking on the most entrenched politician in all of Texas politics, and the longest tenured, active congressman in the United States House of Representatives? Still, I was more attracted to the pastors who supported Steve than I was to Steve, initially. I was particularly impressed by one pastor who was very committed to Steve. His church was one of the fastest growing congregations in Houston. I found him to be a man of courage and integrity. Though only a small portion of Pearland was in Steve Stockman's Congressional District, I accepted an invitation to serve on the Executive Committee of the Southeast Texas Pastors' Roundtable.

A Passion For Restoring America

As I got to know Steve and his lovely wife, Patti, I grew to love and admire them greatly. I discovered Steve to be a man who held a deep passion for restoring America to her Christian heritage. He was running for Congress because he believed it to be God's will for his life. After watching the downward spiral of the country he loved, Steve decided,

"Enough was Enough."

He began his quest in 1990. He conducted a door-to-door campaign with all volunteers. Though he was a Republican, he received no support and very little encouragement from his party. He was defeated in the Republican Primary.

Instead of giving up and walking away, Steve began focusing on the 1992 elections. He decided to network pastors and encourage them to get their members to the polls. Steve believed that people with biblical values would naturally vote conservatively. At least for the present, when it comes to the party platforms, the Republican party is clearly the party that most reflects traditional family values.

Steve devoted all his energies in the 1992 campaign to mobilizing Christians to the polls. In July of 1992, Steve's campaign sponsored a Mobilizing Morality Conference, featuring a number of outstanding, conservative men of God, like Dr. Jerry Falwell, Dr. Peter Marshall and Dr. Tim LaHaye. A number of our church members attended the conference and were exposed to Steve Stockman. As always, the conference focused on issues of morality, from a biblical perspective. Other conferences were held throughout the Congressional district in an effort to inform Christians of the issues, and motivate them to register and vote their convictions.

Making Political Headway

By the end of the 1992 campaign, people began to notice this neophyte Christian politician, Steve Stockman. We knew that Steve was making headway when Jack Brooks began publicly attacking him. Though outspent by a margin of six to one, Steve managed to garner forty-four percent of the votes in 1992. Suddenly, people began to believe the mighty Jack Brooks could be defeated.

Encouraged by the numbers, Steve and Patti turned their focus to 1994. I believe the greatest human expression of true biblical faith is persistence. If you really believe that God has spoken to you regarding something He intends to bring to pass, you will not quit until it becomes a reality. If a person ever ceases to pursue a goal, it is proof that he never really believed the goal would be accomplished. Persistence is an outward expression of faith. Steve never quit.

We became close friends and allies in the process. In the course of time, many of us around Steve began to share his vision of being elected. To his great credit and to God's great glory, Steve kept pursuing his goal. Though Christians often let Steve down by not supporting his Mobilizing Morality Conferences very well, he refused to change his strategy. Even political advisors from the Republican Party discouraged Steve's heavy dependence on the Christian vote, but he would not be deterred. On election night in 1994, the impossible suddenly became possible. The run of forty-two consecutive years in Washington finally came to an end for the formidable Jack Brooks. Steve Stockman, a conservative Christian, running as a Republican, received fifty-two percent of the vote. As unlikely as it seems, one of the strongholds of union-dominated Democratic politics went Republican, as Christian people in his district, standing with other conservatives, voted Steve Stockman into office.

A Christian Oath Of Office

On January 4, 1995, I had the privilege of being invited by Congressman Steve Stockman to Washington, D.C., where about 150 close friends and supporters, participated in an informal, Christian, "swearing-in" ceremony. It was my honor to administer the following Christian oath of office to Congressman Steve Stockman:

> I, Steve Stockman, do solemnly commit before the Lord God of Heaven and these witnesses, that I will support and defend the Constitution of the United States of America against all enemies, foreign and domestic; that I will bear true faith and allegiance to the same; that I take this obligation as a charge from the God of Heaven and the constituents that I serve, willingly and without any mental reservation, recognizing that there is no authority except that which God has established. As an elected official I recognize that I am God's servant, placed in office to do good. With the aid of the Almighty and the guidance of His Spirit, I will faithfully discharge the duties of the office on which I am about to enter, in a way that will honor His Son. So help me God.

I also prayed the following prayer, which is based on Psalm 20, as we concluded the informal swearing-in:

> May the Lord answer you when you are in distress; may the name of the God of Jacob protect you. May he send you help from the sanctuary and grant you support from Zion. May he remember all your sacrifices and accept your burnt offerings. May he give you the desire of your heart and make all your plans succeed. We will shout for joy when you are victorious and will lift up our

banners in the name of our God. May the Lord grant all your requests. Now I know that the Lord saves his anointed; he answers him from his holy heaven with the saving power of his right hand. Some trust in chariots and some in horses, but we trust in the name of the Lord our God. They are brought to their knees and fall, but we rise up and stand firm. O Lord, save the King! Answer us when we call!

Dr. Paul Weyrich, President and CEO of NET, reported to his national television audience, after attending this informal "swearing-in" ceremony:

...Here it seemed to me was what the political process in America is all about. It isn't about ego driven celebrities making pompous speeches. It isn't about getting your fifteen minutes of fame in the media. It isn't about who can out-debate the other on the house floor. It is about ordinary people deciding to do something about their government. It is about a young, down-to-earth, middle class professional giving up six years of his time to run three times until successful in defeating one of the most powerful and nasty politicians ever to have stalked this capital...

During the course of the events that preceded the election victory of Steve Stockman, I received a call from an old friend, Dr. Stephen Hotze. He is an Allergist, with a large medical practice in far West Houston. He is also very active in conservative politics.

Steve and I go way back. In 1968 he and I served as president and vice president, respectively, of the Greater Houston Area Association of Student Body Presidents. As the presidents of our respective high school student bodies, we held a mutual love for our country. One day we were discussing our common concern that the "bad" kids who were burning flags, dodging the draft, and taking drugs, were getting all the attention in the press. We decided there needed to be an "Up With America" rally in Houston. Several months and many miles later, we sponsored a parade through downtown Houston, followed by a huge rally at the downtown convention center. Texas Governor John Connally was our featured guest. A young black man, who was then the President of Boy's Nation, also spoke that day. His name was Alan Keyes, a candidate for president in 1996. The entire event proved to be a great success.

Though we were very close friends in high school, we lost touch pursuing degrees and dreams during the years that followed. In 1983, the doctor received a lot of media attention around Houston, as he helped sponsor a referendum to repeal a city ordinance in Houston granting special recognition to gays. I was living in Alabama at the time, but my parents kept me informed of my friend's activities.

Renewing Our Friendship

In 1994, we renewed our friendship. During the twenty-plus years since our earlier friendship, both of us made important commitments of our lives to the Lordship of Christ. The doctor learned of my political activism in Pearland and with the Stockman campaign, and he asked if I would be willing to help him organize a Houston Area Pastors' Roundtable. He offered to do all of the organization and work if I would be willing to link my name and influence with pastors, and share my testimony at a breakfast meeting. I agreed and the meeting was scheduled.

Advertised as an informal information gathering-meeting, we planned for 125 pastors and church leaders. To our great delight, over 170 attended. With the 1994 election only a few months away, pastors showed a great interest in learning how to mobilize their people to action. Our city manager and police chief both accompanied me to the meeting and spoke briefly to the pastors. The doctor provided an abundance of literature for the pastors, as well as copies of David Barton's video "The Foundation Of American Government." That morning, the Greater Houston Area Pastors' Roundtable was born.

Two more luncheons were scheduled, featuring such notable speakers as educator Thaddeus Lott and pastor, Dr. Jerry Falwell. With every meeting, more pastors were enlisted and encouraged to register their members to vote and perform their Christian civic duty. All of us had a growing sense that this was a supernatural movement of our God that transcended any one's ability to organize or mobilize. That is not meant to discredit Dr. Hotze, and his staff of paid and volunteer workers, who worked tirelessly to contact pastors and organize the events. Faith and works go hand in hand in every successful endeavor. Clearly, God was doing something that exceeded our abilities.

A Conservative Swing

Houston and Harris County, like the rest of the country, experienced an incredible move toward conservatism in the 1994 election. However, in Harris County, the results were demonstrably more Christian conservative in nature. In the courts of Harris County, fifty-two liberal judges and judicial candidates were defeated by conservatives. Perhaps the most gratifying victory of all was the election of a committed Christian, John Devine. John defeated Ann Richard's liberal judicial appointee, Judge Eileen O'Neil, who in 1992 declared a 100 foot space of public property around an abortuary, to be a "Gospel-Free" zone. Because of this judge's ruling, dozens of pro-lifers were arrested and placed in the Harris County Jail during the Republican National Convention, for the crime of exercising their constitutional rights of free speech and assembly. We like to refer to the new judge as God's "Divine" choice to replace Ann Richard's poor appointment. Truly, God has the last word.

Plans for the future include taking the message of Christian involvement in civil affairs across the South. I believe that the American culture has been under attack for the past thirty years, largely due to many Christians withdrawing from the process. As more pastors are informed and mobilized, they can in turn inform and mobilize their people to return to the civil arena. There is an exciting truth contained in our Lord's analogy of salt and light, and the role of Christians in society. It does not take much salt to season a whole meal, and a small amount of light can transform a darkened room. It is time for the Church to say "Enough is Enough."

"Providence has given to our people the choice of their rulers, and it is the duty, as well as the privilege and interest of our Christian Nation to select and prefer Christians for their rulers."

-John Jay (October 12, 1816)
First Chief Justice of
the United States Supreme Court

Chapter Twenty-One

Pray, And Grab A Hoe

During World War II, the soldiers learned to express their understanding of the important biblical teaching: Faith without works is dead." (James 2;19), by saying, "Pray, and pass the ammunition." In East Texas, the same concept is expressed with the old adage, "Pray, and grab a hoe."

It is time for Christians in America to..." Pray, and grab a hoe." The longer I live, the more I realize that God has woven the principle of sowing and reaping throughout the natural world. Everything in this world that matters is effected by the law of sowing and reaping. By that, I mean everything we do in life has a delayed response. For example, if you plant a seed of corn in the ground, you do not expect an ear of corn to grow immediately. You plant today, but you reap tomorrow. If you fail to plant today, you will not reap tomorrow. Everything that matters depends upon this law.

Life in the fifties was good because American society embraced the Judeo-Christian ethic for many generations prior to the fifties. In the sixties, a different cultural seed was planted. Now, we are harvesting the fruit of the evil, cultural seed with an abundant harvest of evil. The future for America will be even bleaker unless a different seed is planted.

I believe the only hope for the restoration of this nation is the church. Christians across America must finally say, "Enough is Enough." America will not be changed from the top down, but rather from the bottom up. Ronald Reagan was a great American President. He stood up for traditional family values and wrote a book decrying abortion. Under his leadership, America was restored to a role of world leadership and the communist stranglehold was broken. The "Great Satan," the mighty Soviet Union, was dismantled after seventy years of dominating one-third of the world's population, as Ronald Reagan courageously stood up to the Soviets.

As great as Ronald Reagan was as a leader, he could not restore America to her Christian heritage. That is because true change can only come from the bottom up. It begins in small towns across America, like

241

Pearland. It will not happen until Christians begin to stand up to be counted, by informing themselves of the issues that confront America, and then going to the polls and expressing their convictions.

The American political system is a game of numbers. Whoever has the most votes wins. For more than three decades, we Christians have been failing to exercise our influence because we have failed to even show up to vote. Because of our neglect, a relatively small, but radical coalition of pro-abortion, pro-homosexual, anti-religion secular humanists have been able to elect their candidates and shape the culture of America. I believe the vast majority of Americans are conservative in their life-style and their politics. I believe the vast majority of Americans still believe in God and want a country based on biblical values. I believe most Americans are ready to stand with anyone who will say, "Enough is Enough." The liberal theories of the sixties have not worked.

There are several things that you can do right where you live, if you agree, "Enough is Enough."

First, register everyone you can to vote. It is not necessary to tell Christians how to vote. If they are informed of the issues, most will vote their biblical convictions, and America will be restored. Many Christians do not realize how easy it is to register voters. In the State of Texas, to become a voter registrar, all that is required is for you to go to your county courthouse, fill out an application, and receive a certificate of appointment to serve as a volunteer deputy registrar. You will then be given voter registration forms and the authority to register voters. Preceding every major election, we set up tables around the church and encourage our members to register to vote.

Second, enlist godly men and women who are skillful leaders, to run for office. Christians need to run for the school board, the city council, county government, state government and national office. Daniel Webster was correct when he said, "Whatever makes men good Christians, makes them good citizens." [113]

John Jay was correct when he said, "Providence has given to our people the choice of their rulers, and it is the duty as well as the privilege of and interest of our Christian nation to select and prefer Christians as their rulers." [114]

I believe it is time for Christian men and women to stand up and be counted.

Third, Christians need to get involved in the political process at every level. Few Christians have any working knowledge of how a party platform is constructed, and consequently they do not understand how much influence they can exert by participating in the process. Christians must acquaint themselves with the political party structure in America.

They must then; "Pray, and Grab a Hoe."

In every polling precinct, immediately following an election primary, on the same evening, a precinct convention is held. To participate in a precinct convention, you are required to vote in the primary. Typically, very few voters attend, county, state and national conventions, at the precinct level. Christians must acquaint themselves with this process and get involved. A small number of voters, with strong Christian convictions, can pass resolutions that reflect their biblical values and make a powerful impact.

Fourth, Christians must vote and recruit others to vote. Early voting removes the excuse of being too busy. Today, the law allows voters to avoid the lengthy lines and possible scheduling conflicts of election day by providing voters the opportunity to vote at their convenience before election day. This provides busy people ample opportunity to exercise their right to express their convictions. Typically, early voting dates include at least one Sunday afternoon. A growing number of churches elect to bus their members to the polls on that day to vote. If we fail to vote, we forfeit the right to complain about the results.

Fifth, churches need to organize a committee of laypeople whose sole charge is to keep moral concerns before the congregation. A number of good names for the committee have surfaced over the past few years. For example: "The Moral Action Committee," "Moral Concerns Committee," "The Christian Action Committee," etc. In our church, we refer to the committee as the "Moral Action Ministry Team."

These people keep the pastor and staff abreast of local and national moral concerns. In addition, this committee is an excellent resource to help register voters and distribute information about moral concerns. Every church should have a standing Moral Action Ministry Team, or something similar, with the charge of keeping the church family informed regarding moral concerns. If your church does not have a Moral Action Ministry Team, why not approach your pastor about organizing one? Why not volunteer to assist in the project?

Undergirding all of the above must be prevailing prayer. James reminds us: "The prayer of a righteous man is powerful and effective" (James 5;16). In the first page of this book, I remarked that Nehemiah fasted and prayed with a broken heart. Those three ingredients of fasting, praying and brokenness are indispensable if we are to restore America to her Christian heritage. I have heard it said many times; We must pray as if it all depends on God, and work as if it all depends on us. I believe that describes the mixture of faith and works that God honors...if it is done with a broken heart. The Psalmist writes: "Those who sow in tears will reap with songs of joy..., carrying sheaves with him" (Psalm 126:5-6). It is time to "Pray, and Grab a Hoe."

Endnotes

1   *America's God And Country*, William Federer, page 703.
2   *The Rebirth of America*, "The Bible and the Dawn of the American Dream," published by The Author S. DeMoss Foundation, page 36.
3   *America's Christian History, The Untold Story*, Gary DeMar, page 52.
4   Ibid, page 58.
5   Ibid, page 58.
6   Ibid, page 59.
7   Ibid, pages 60-61.
8   Ibid, page 65.
9   Ibid, page 69.
10 Ibid, page 73.
11 Ibid, page 73.
12 *America's God And Country*, William Federer, page 634..
13 Ibid, page 460.
14 Ibid, page 460.
15 Ibid, note #82, page 716.
16 Ibid, page 101.
17 Ibid, pages 248.
18 Ibid, pages 199-200.
19 Ibid, note #32, page 785.
20 Ibid, page 10-11.
21 Ibid, page 411.
22 Ibid, page 318.
23 Ibid, page 669.
24 Ibid, page 273.
25 Ibid, page 274.
26 Ibid, page 274.
27 Ibid, pages 651-652.
28 Ibid, page 661.
29 *America's Christian History, The Untold Story*, Gary DeMar, pg. 101.
30 Ibid, page 103.
31 *America's God And Country*, William Federer, page 190.
32 Ibid, pages 204-206.
33 *The Supreme Court Reborn: The Constitutional Revolution in the Age of Roosevelt by William E. Lauchtenburg*, Oxford Press, 90-92 pages.
34 *America; To Pray Or Not To Pray*, David Barton, Preface.
35 Engel v. Vitale, 1962.
36 Ibid.
37 *America's God And Country*, William Federer, page 654.
38 Engel v. Vitale, 1962.
39 Ibid.
40 *America's God And Country*, William Federer, pages 10-11.
41 *The Myth of Separation*, David Barton, page 15.
42 *America's God And Country*, William Federer, page 325.
43 *The Myth of Separation*, David Barton, pages 11-13.
44 *America's God And Country*, William Federer, page 347.

45 *The Index of Leading Cultural Indicators*, William Bennett, Introduction, page 8.
46 Ibid, pages 9-10.
47 *The Devaluing of America*, William Bennett, Preface, Updated Edition.
48 *America's God And Country*, William Federer, page 205.
59 *The Battle For The Mind*, Tim LaHaye, page 33.
50 Ibid, pages 80-91.
51 Ibid, page 96.
52 *Whatever Happened To The American Dream*, Larry Burkett, page 39.
53 Ibid, page 99.
54 *See! I Told You So*, Rush Limbaugh, pages 172-73.
55 Ibid, page 173.
56 *America's God And Country*, William Federer, page 281.
57 *The Coming Economic Earthquake*, Larry Burkett, page 33.
58 Ibid, page 34.
59 *The Mike Richards News Digest*, June Issue, page 1.
60 *Standing Tall*, Steve Farrar, pages 162-164.
61 *America's God And Country*, William Federer, pages 636-637.
62 *The Battle For The Mind*, Tim LaHaye, page 87.
63 *Hollywood vs. America*, Michael Medved, page 52.
64 Ibid, page 52.
65 Ibid, page 56.
66 Ibid, page 56.
67 Ibid, page 59.
68 Ibid, pages 66-67.
69 *"Many Are At Fault For Insurance Woe,"* Washington Post, Feb. 24, 1986, by T.R. Reid, The American Hour, O.S. Guinness, pg. 363.
70 Ibid, pages 363-364.
71 *America's God And Country*, William Federer, pages 411-412.
72 *The Battle For The Mind*, Tim LaHaye, page 87.
73 *The American Hour*, O.S. Guinness, page 339.
74 Ibid, page 340.
75 Ibid, pages 340-341.
76 *Hollywood vs. America*, Michael Medved, page 23.
77 Ibid page 23.
78 Ibid, pages 26-27.
79 Ibid, page 27.
80 Ibid, page 28.
81 Ibid, page 31
82 Ibid, page 77.
83 Ibid, page 77.
84 Ibid, page 97.
85 Ibid, page 98.
86 Ibid. page 98.
87 Ibid, page 98.
88 Ibid, page102.
89 Ibid, page 102.

90 Ibid, page 102.
91 Ibid, page 103.
92 *Battle For The Mind,* Tim LaHaye, pages 87-88.
93 *Family Under Siege,* George Grant, page 156.
94 *"The Gay Agenda,"* a video produced by "The Report," (Lancaster, Calif.).
95 *The Family Under Siege,* George Grant, page 166.
96 Ibid, pages 166-167.
97 Ibid, page 177.
98 *Standing Tall,* Steve Farrar, page 115.
99 Ibid, pages 141-142.
100 *The Devaluing of America,* William Bennett, Preface.
101 Ibid.
102 *"Struggling To Save Our Kids,"* Fortune Magazine, August 10, 1992.
103 *The Devaluing of America,* William Bennett, page 34.
104 *Against The Night,* Chuck Colson, page 73.
105 *The Feminine Mystique,* Betty Friedan, 1963, page IX.
106 Ibid.
107 Ibid.
108 *Whatever Happened to the Human Race,* C. Everett Koop, M.D. and Francis A. Schaeffer. page 13.
109 Ibid, page 13-14.
110 Pearland Journal, August 4, 1993.
111 *"A Time For Action,"* Pearland Journal.
112 Pearland Journal and Pearland Reporter
113 *America's God and Country,* William Federer, page 669.
114 Ibid, page 318.